Golden Apples
for
Golden-Agers

D1282205

Golden Apples
for
Golden-Agers

DEVOTIONALS WRITTEN BY AND FOR SENIORS

"A word fitly spoken is like apples of gold in pictures of silver."
—Proverbs 25:11

Leroy Brightup and Eva M. Brightup

iUniverse, Inc.
Bloomington

Golden Apples for Golden-Agers
Devotionals Written by and for Seniors

iUniverse Star
an iUniverse, Inc. imprint

iUniverse books may be ordered through booksellers or by contacting:

iUniverse
1663 Liberty Drive
Bloomington, IN 47403
www.iuniverse.com
1-800-Authors (1-800-288-4677)

ISBN: 978-1-938908-00-2 (sc)
ISBN: 978-1-938908-01-9 (e)

Library of Congress Control Number: 2012904512

Printed in the United States of America

iUniverse rev. date: 3/21/2012

Preface

Being old is something new for us—not that we didn't expect it, but we have never been here before!

Those of us who are of an older age may be tempted to assume that we've seen it all before and that there is no more growing or learning to be done; that life is just daily, repetitious circling until we spiral down to the end. I, Leroy, was brought up short when I read a devotional written by an eighty-year-old man, (see first devotional) in which he acknowledged that God had been dealing with him about his poor attitude. A lightbulb came on in my head as I realized that oldsters have to deal with some special issues, and one is never too old to be coached by God toward more Christlike living.

Seniors share many things in common (e.g., changes in financial resources and sense of purpose and usefulness, health issues, many types of losses, end-of-life issues). Because both Eva and I draw our daily strength from scriptures and spiritual readings, it became clear that honest reporting and reflection by retired and aging Christian fellow travelers would be helpful and encouraging. Thus, the vision was born to assemble this collection of first-person experiences and resources for coping with the senior years in a

Christian way. In this book, golden-agers reflect on life as they find it now. Many are in their eighties; several are in their nineties.

The devotionals reflect diversity and have not been numbered or dated. Reading them can profitably begin anywhere. Except as noted, scriptural quotations and paraphrases are from the King James Version of the Holy Bible.

We are extremely grateful to the numerous writers who have submitted material. We also are appreciative to several publishers for permission to reprint material. Without their assistance, this devotional manual would not have come into existence. (End pages provide full bibliographical data for sources used with permission.)

Many of our previous associates have already gone to their eternal reward. Those of us who have the opportunity to live longer also have the opportunity to increase in spiritual maturity. We hope you will take from our baskets "an apple a day" to help keep stagnation away.

Leroy and Eva M. Brightup

Contents

Basket 1
Receiving Grace

Attitude

Bible Reading: Philippians 2:5–13

For several years, as a part of my job responsibility, I traveled the nation, speaking and leading seminars on Christian education. Invariably, sometime during my presentation, I worked in this illustration about leadership: "There are three steps to success in any endeavor. The first is attitude." (Pause.) "The second is attitude." (Pause.) "And the third is attitude!"

This is true. Your attitude in life makes all the difference. An e-mail received some months ago contained this apt sentence: "The only thing that is truly yours that no one can control or take from you is your attitude." I believe I have generally been a person "with a positive attitude, enthusiastic about life," in spite of some difficult times of testing. But about a year ago I became convicted about my attitude, which seemed to have become more negative. So, I asked the Lord to change my attitude. And he did.

The Bible reading today sets a high standard and challenge for the Christian when it begins with this emphatic statement in Philippians 2:5 (NIV): "Your attitude should be the same as that of Christ Jesus." Wow! His was a sacrificial and servant attitude, submissive to the Father. There is only one way to be like that. It is not from our own efforts. Rather, it is to follow the admonition of the apostle Paul when he said, "You were taught … to be made new in the attitude of your minds; and to put on the new self, created to be like God in true righteousness and holiness" (Ephesians 4:22–24 [NIV]).

—Robert A. Crandall, *Fruit*, vol. 49, no. 4, p.27
(Used with permission)

Song: "May the Mind of Christ, My Savior"

A Suggested Prayer: Search my heart, O God, and see if there is any wrong attitude in me and lead me in the way everlasting.

A Chance Find?

Bible Reading: Psalm 42:11

Yesterday was hard! Today's been hard, too. We've struggled through the day, both of us so exhausted [that] every movement, every thought has been an effort. Waves of nausea and acute weariness have swept over me from time to time, threatening to overpower me. Then they pass only to return later. Strange.

When I walked past my wall calendar in the kitchen this morning, I sighed as I noted all the commitments I had made months earlier, some to be met either before [my husband] Luverne's scheduled [prostate cancer] surgery in six days' time and others shortly afterwards. I wondered how I ever would be able to fulfill them.

After breakfast, while the clothes were tumbling in the dryer and the water was swishing the dishes clean in the dishwasher, I assembled all the boxes of Christmas decorations. Opening the first one labeled "candles," spying a strip of parchment lying on the bottom, and being curious, I lifted it out. On it, Janet, during her high school years when she was designing wall plaques, had inscribed in calligraphy: "So give me the strength I need."

I stared at the words. I had found a prayer I could pray. Taking the paper, I taped it to the refrigerator door. And praying that prayer as I worked, I did manage to get most of the Christmas decorations in place for all our various scheduled festivities.

—Mildred Tengbom, *Moving*, p. 7
(Used with permission)

Song: "Day by Day"

A Suggested Prayer: Thank you, Lord, for unexpected surprises, especially those that sustain us in difficult moments.

A Question of Angels

Bible Reading: Luke 2:1–10

On a recent trip to Paris, my wife, Laura, and I were unable to stay in our favorite hotel. Instead, we moved to a new neighborhood, quiet and small.

Our first night there, we wandered the unfamiliar streets, dark and deserted. We were lost and could not find our hotel.

Then I heard a voice. "Where are you from?" I turned around and met a young, blond, blue-eyed man, dressed in light clothing—not your typical Parisian.

"America," I said.

"I know that," he said. "But where?"

"Kansas."

He looked into my eyes, broke into a smile, extended his hand, and said, "Do not be afraid."

I shook his hand and thanked him. Laura and I walked on. In a few moments, I looked back. He was gone.

We knew immediately that he had been an angel. His suddenly appearing and vanishing; his atypical demeanor; his simple, biblical command. We walked another few yards, turned, and there was our hotel.

Extraordinary, right?

Yes. Except, I wondered, what had this angel really done for us? He hadn't solved our problem; we were still lost when he left us.

But I knew the answer to my question as soon as I had asked it. He had delivered faith's abiding message: God is with us.

God is with us even in the most mundane matters of life. He is with us, whether we sense him or not. He is with us exactly when we need him.

His angels, when they appear, are merely instruments of his care. They are tangible reminders that we are not alone in our travels, that we are never truly lost.

His angels come always to proclaim, "Do not be afraid."

—Arlice Davenport, Wichita, KS

Song: "How Firm a Foundation"

A Suggested Prayer: O Lord, help us not to fear along life's journeys, but put our trust unfailingly in your providence and care.

The Written Word

Bible Reading: Romans 12:5–6

In Romans 12:6 (LB), Paul writes: "God has given each of us the ability to do certain things well. ..." Then in subsequent verses, he lists several of these gifts. Growing up on a farm, I was gifted with love of the great outdoors exclusively, until learning to read in the third grade. From that point forward, my love of the outdoors remained, but when forced inside, my new gift of reading was exercised. By my twenties, life's circumstances moved me away from the outdoors and related activities, into a world built around the written word.

From an early age I loved to sit and listen to the stories told by the "old people." By the 1970s, much of my spare time was spent expanding on and converting these stories into written form. I eventually published two rather lengthy books about family, from their earliest known roots through my grandchildren's generation.

I found this to be a nearly thankless task. Almost everyone is interested in outdoors and sports activities and building things, but few have interest in recording and sharing family history. Many were the times, while taking a break from these writings, that I would stand at the back door looking across our yard, wondering why I was wasting so much of my time on something that seemingly no one cared about. But then, this quiet, gentle, inner voice (the Holy Spirit) would remind me this work was another of God's gifts and was my way of bringing glory to his holy name.

Within the past year, my outreach has been expanded to include sharing these lifelong memories weekly in my hometown newspaper—and now in this devotional. Isn't it great that even in our twilight years, we can continue to exercise God's gifts?

—Derl Williams, Wichita, KS

Song: "A Beautiful Life"

A Suggested Prayer: God, keep us ever mindful of the gifts received and opportunities that come our way to glorify your name.

My Amazing God

Bible Reading: Psalm 139:13–16

How could I ever reject a God who knew every delicate part of me while I was being formed in my mother's womb? You watched me as I was being woven together, and even before I was born you saw every day of my life recorded in your books. I am amazed that you would know when I would sin against you and then you would know when I would kneel at an altar of prayer and come to you and ask forgiveness for that sin and begin to follow you. Every step of my life, from that moment it was first recorded until now, at age eighty-eight, has been directed by you. What an amazing God!

How could I know that God would bless me with a husband who was called by God to minister for him for sixty years? What an amazing God who, while I was still in my mother's womb, saw me as the person to serve alongside this man of God and raise five of our children and help raise three others. What an amazing God!

—Betty Robinson, Wichita, KS

Song: "My Savior's Love"

A Suggested Prayer: Psalm 139:23–24 (NIV). "Search me, O God, and know my heart; test me and know my anxious thoughts. See if there is any offensive way in me, and lead me [even at this senior age] in the path of everlasting life."

Joy Is a Precious Gift from God

Bible Reading: Psalm 19:8; Romans 15:13

What is joy? How does one find it? Why do I want it?

Those are questions that deserve an answer because joy is at the heart of being a Christian. Does joy mean that one is always happy? Not exactly. Let me explain:

Joy is the Tie that Holds Love and Peace Together!

1. *Joy is a choice.* We can choose to face what comes in life with confidence or with defeat. We can cooperate with circumstances, or we can complain. We can be pleasant, or we can be rude. We can make the best of situations, or we can be defeated.

2. *Joy is not dependent* on the events and circumstances of life. Our attitudes and acceptance depend on our individual will. It does not depend on "if only" or "as soon as." Joy can be experienced here and now.

3. *Joy is free*, but it *is not* cheap. It costs patience, and it takes endurance, and it grows when it's shared. But it diminishes when it is used selfishly.

4. *Joy is a precious possession* of happiness. In spiritual terms, it is the result of being attuned to God and his wisdom and care.

5. *Joy is a source of strength* that God supplies.

6. *Joy is a promise* that is given to the *Christian*.

7. *Joy is the result* of the Christian life because God is there in any situation, and Jesus is our Savior.

—Faye McCoy, *One Generation*, p. 18
(Used with permission)

Song: "I Have the Joy, Joy Down in My Heart"

A Suggested Prayer: Joy wells up within me whenever I pause to contemplate all you have done for me. I pray I will share this joy with others as much as I can.

Receiving Gracefully

Bible Reading: Matthew 9:27–31

As a wife and mother, I enjoyed cooking, housekeeping, laundry, and chauffeuring. I tried to live by the adage "It is more blessed to give than to receive."

But a few months ago the tables were turned. I was forced to be in bed or a recliner, waited on for even the simplest needs. It was a humbling experience to be on the receiving end, over and over, as I became helpless. But my helplessness also brought one blessing after another from the hand of the Lord.

My husband became housekeeper and nurse. He learned to prepare meals and do laundry. He was the lone shopper, heading to the store with a list and searching the aisles for items. He purchased and dispensed my medications and more than once drove me to the hospital emergency room late at night or in early morning.

Learning to receive gratefully and without embarrassment became a joy as neighbors in our apartment community appeared at our door every other evening with wonderful meals, hot and appetizing, for an entire month. "Thank you" became overused, but there was no other way except a verbal thanks to repay those kindnesses.

It may be more blessed to give than to receive, but receiving in an hour of need is a blessing beyond compare.

—Marjorie Crisman, *Fruit*, vol. 49, no.3, p. 83
(Used with permission)

Song: "Count Your Blessings"

A Suggested Prayer: Thank you, Lord, for Christian sisters and brothers who respond to your promptings and come to our aid in time of need.

Basket 2
Growing Older

Reverse Aging

Bible Reading: Isaiah 46:3–4

A recent movie titled *The Strange Case of Benjamin Button* depicted the fiction of a person appearing to be old when born but who daily grew younger. A novel idea—that we might undo the ravages and changes that the years have worked on our bodies and lives! To be young again sounds welcome, but do I really want that, even if medical science could actually bring it about?

Growing older has its difficulties, but I don't hanker to be younger again, not when I recall carefully the turmoil and anguish of youth—the teen years, with acne, raging hormones, peer pressure, and search for self-identity; fear and feelings of being a misfit; and grappling with career choices. I recall in early adulthood the financial pressures; trying to succeed in the eyes of my employers; working two jobs; and the time pressures of raising a young family with dental appointments, music lessons, Bluebirds, school programs, and soccer and baseball practice and games.

This season of life seems more settled and wonderfully rich—with freedom from needing to impress anyone; with opportunity to manage my own schedule; with time to reflect on good memories of those who opened opportunities for me as I traveled my career path; with time to enjoy my grandchildren with all their energy and potential; and with a few of life's questions answered.

I have no interest in reverse-aging and returning to the days of youth. I like the days of maturity. I am willing to settle for the relative calm of aging and accept the challenges that come with it.

—Leroy Brightup

Song: "Abide with Me"

A Suggested Prayer: Lord, your abiding presence gives us comfort in old age, even as you have been our strength and shield through younger years.

Stumbling into His Arms

Bible Reading: Psalm 94:17–19

It was cold. It was Paris. It was forty years ago. I recall the details vividly because my camera preserved the elderly couple on film. Their black-and-white image first emerged in my darkroom in the late 1960s. The image hasn't faded, and neither has its power to evoke memories of Paris and my encounter long ago.

The old man and woman sat on a sidewalk bench where their faces caught the sun. They leaned into one another for support and warmth. Their clothes indicated a low socioeconomic class. Their faces indicated a hard life. I considered their ages and guessed they had experienced two world wars. Perhaps she had watched Nazis march down Avenue des Champs-Elysees, while he endured skirmishes on some battlefield.

They were utterly alone and oblivious to passersby, who were just as oblivious to the old couple. When they slowly stirred to leave, they rose with difficulty. Each helped the other break loose from their rest, stand up, and take tentative steps into a swirl of indifferent pedestrians. They shuffled off, reliant on each other's support. A fragile companion wasn't much to lean on, but it was all either of them seemed to have.

Now that I am old enough to detect the first signs of my physical unsteadiness, I think about what and whom I can lean on. In times of distress, when I feel alone or when I stumble, no support is more steadfast or more comforting than Jesus Christ. Even in my daily walk, his welcoming arms are around me to comfort and shield.

—Norman Carr, Wichita, KS

Song: "Leaning on the Everlasting Arms"

A Suggested Prayer: Dear God, you sent your Son to right a fallen world and to lift those who would believe. Teach us to cling to your unfailing love, even as our steps sometimes falter. Lead us into Christ and into his everlasting arms.

Loss of Memory

Bible Reading: Hebrews 10:11–17

For many of us, a dimness of past events (or even present duties!) seems to come along with age. An elderly lady was asked by her pastor whether she ever thought about the hereafter. She replied that she thought about it a lot, that she would often come into a room and think "What am I here after?"

Although my brother remembers birthdays and other family events clearly, I have few specific memories of my childhood or even of the middle years of a busy career and raising children.

We seniors wish for better memory, but in 2006 a woman named Jill Price was featured on *20/20* and *Good Morning America* as the "Woman Who Can't Forget." She can recall literally every day of her life and its happenings, from youth up. She remembers what she had to eat as well as what world happenings took place on any given day. What a burden!

Who wants to remember all the anger, hurts, and pain from the past—all the hurtful tangles with siblings and associates; all the names we've been called; all the sins, mistakes, and errors; childhood punishments; and jilted love of youthful romance? Even Jill Price reports experiencing a good deal of pain because of her inability to forget difficult moments.

Some things shouldn't be forgotten, such as one's wedding (and especially the anniversary!). Some things can't be forgotten because they are so deeply imbedded in life and memory, such as the horrors of war. But even *God* can't remember some things. He forgets our sins and remembers them against us no more (Heb. 8:12).

The one who can't forget finds it hard to forgive. The incident is never buried in the past but always fresh on his or her mind. Be thankful that God allows some things to pass into oblivion.

—Leroy Brightup

Song: "Freely, Freely"

Prayer Suggestion: Pray for God to reveal to you any harbored thought or unforgiveness that needs to be released, to be remembered no more.

Things to Do after Sixty-Two

Bible Reading: Psalm 92:14

Is it true that life really ends at sixty-two? I thought the psalmist promised us seventy and sometimes eighty years! Inflation isn't eating years, too, is it? Life does seem to end at sixty-two for some people. They reach retirement age and find that all they have planned to do is rock and watch television.

Are you interested in creative ways to spend your retirement? Here are four possibilities I came across in the Bible.

Build a boat. Don't laugh! Noah was six hundred years old, according to Genesis 7:6, when the flood came. He'd started building his boat after he was past his five hundredth birthday. Your boat won't be as large as his was, so what's to prevent you from starting your sketches later today?

Water may not appeal to you. If that is the case, try climbing mountains. Soreness will give way to pleasure (eventually). Caleb was eighty-five when he began learning the sport. His story is found in Joshua 14:10–12, if you would like more information.

Waiting for something easier? Try being a tour guide. Did you realize Moses was eighty when he accepted the responsibility for leading the Israelites on a tour of the wilderness?

If unique is what you seek, get into politics and run for president. Why not? Daniel became "president" in the Persian Empire between his eighth and ninth decades. Age sharpened his skills, instead of impairing them, and brought with it wisdom. Think about it.

—Frank Scurry, *Refreshings*, p. 224
(Used with permission)

Song: "God of Our Life, through All the Circling Years"

A Suggested Prayer: O, God, "teach us to number our days that we may apply our hearts unto wisdom" (Psalm 90:12).

Age Denial

Bible Reading: Joshua 14:6–13

My father enjoyed telling the story of a long-departed relative who refused to acknowledge among his peers that his age had taken a toll on his body. His boast, "I'm as good a man now as I ever was," usually ended, however, with "except for this elbow and the pain in my hip."

Merchants find a ready market in our reluctance to admit that we are growing older. Advertisements are abundant for women's creams to remove wrinkles, and other age-defying treatments. I recall my dismay at having to get bifocals in my college years and hearing aids in mid-life. I was afraid I'd be mistaken for an old person!

However, I experienced a great deal of freedom when I acknowledged to myself that my life and relationships were greatly improved with hearing aids. I became thankful for the availability of these devices and lost my self-consciousness about how they appeared to others.

In the abovementioned Bible reading, Caleb essentially says, "I'm as good a man as I ever was," but it's not an idle boast. While admitting his advanced age (eighty-five), clearly he was ready and anxious to take up additional challenges. He asked to be assigned a portion of the promised land, which still remained to be conquered. Even in old age, he remained interested and invested in life and found new opportunity and energy to pursue a long-awaited dream.

Some try to ignore birthdays or keep them secret, as if old age were a disease. I'm a proud oldster. I've reached a peace with aging. (It's better than the alternative!) I'm thankful for each new day that extends my life. I rest in God's grace to accompany me each step of the way.

—Leroy Brightup

Song: "Amazing Grace"

A Suggested Prayer: God, forgive my grumbling about all I have lost and instead, give me a spirit of gratefulness for the help I receive.

Amazing Grace

Bible Reading: Psalm 23

One of the good things about living a long time is that the shelves of our minds are full of memories that we can take out, turn over and over, and experience once again. Many of those memories are good ones that bring us joy: our childhood home, the pride of each newborn baby, the family fun of watching our children grow and mature, welcoming our children's mates into our hearts and home, becoming grandparents, trips we have taken, good times with friends, and so much more.

Some memories we would like to forget, but God has been showing me lately how precious his grace has been in bad times as well as in good. He was there when we had to say good-bye to our firstborn at birth. A small car accident while we were in college took every penny we had for repairs, but God was there to supply our needs. We experienced the same difficulties all parents face in raising children—angry words, tears, times when we failed to take the time to listen. And, yes, we came through the "parenting our parents" season of our lives, when we sometimes had to encourage them to take steps they didn't want to take.

The good news is that through all of life thus far, I can never think of a time when we didn't sense the grace of God, comforting, guiding, and smoothing the road. It is the amazing grace of God that has guided our journey, and that same grace will see us safely home.

—Eva Brightup

Song: "God Leads Us Along"

A Suggested Prayer: We are grateful for your firm but gentle hands that will be our strength and stability all of our days.

At Ninety-Five

Bible Reading: Psalm 90

She is sitting on a chair in her bedroom. I show her the new pants and blouse. "Try them on, Mom. I got them for you."

"Oh, I don't need any new clothes." She gestures to a pile of folded shirts on her dresser.

"Mom, you are holding up your pants with safety pins. That blouse is worn thin."

She slowly pulls on the new pants, then stands and hitches them over her narrow hips. I help her button the blouse. We both like the results. "You look great, Mom."

She smiles, then announces, "After ninety, the worst is over." We observe a thoughtful silence and then burst into laughter. Eyes twinkling, she says, "Then they dress you. They fix your breakfast."

The good news from [my mom], Irma: if you are over ninety, relax. The worst is over. If you are not, take heart; the best is yet to come.

At ninety-five, my mother knows her memory is impaired but is not particularly bothered about it. She listens to our concerns about her health and safety but does what she pleases. Occasionally, she gets angry, hurts, and grieves. At a recent family gathering, when

I reminded her she was telling us the same story, she scolded me, "Well, I will just be still. I will just crawl under the table." I smarted, as if she had slapped me. But overall, she possesses no self-pity or entitlement and has been released from the burden of ambition. She often says, as her uncle Lem once did, that she now works for "Dolittle and Setmore."

Mother lives, embraced by grace that is as common and generally unnoticed as breath.

—Loretta F. Ross, *Holy Ground*, vol. 19, no. 4, p. 1
(Used with permission)

Song: "Now Thank We All Our God"

A Suggested Prayer: Thank you, Lord, for freedom from many of the pressures we felt in younger years. Help us with the infirmities we now experience.

After Ninety-Three

Bible Reading: Psalm 91

In the poem ["The Dark Night of the Soul"], St. John of the Cross compares the soul to a window. He sees the spiritual journey as the process of cleansing and removal of anything in us that might impede or distort the Light of Christ as it passes through our lives. In this process we become more and more transparent and childlike.

My mother drinks her tea this morning as she watches a squirrel and a cardinal at the feeder. "I am remembering," she says. "I am remembering how when I was a kid and would get upset or complain about something, Pop would say, 'Oh, that ain't nothing to worry about.'"

"Gosh, Mom, that doesn't sound very [empathetic]."

"Well, that is what he would say. 'Oh, that ain't nothing to worry about.'" And she smiles out the window.

I want God to pass through me like a window, to shine on my life as on a meadow. I can ask for it, pray for it, but I think it ain't nothing to worry about. In the end, such childishness is given simply, quietly, in the gracious surrender to growing old.

Mother puts down her teacup and says, "After ninety-three, things get interesting. It is like reading a book backwards. I never understood before why people would look at the end of a book and read it first. It is smooth going. You can do what you want. People don't expect much of you. They think you are childish. They try not to laugh, but you can see they are just dying. I don't let on I know."

—Loretta F. Ross, *Holy Ground*, vol. 19, no.4, p. 6
(Used with permission)

Song: "All the Way My Savior Leads Me"

A Suggested Prayer: In the midst of our worries, Lord, help us to recognize that you have provided the bounty of green pastures and still waters (Psalm 23:2).

Saving

Bible Reading: Psalm 145:1–7

There are a lot of things being sold as antiques these days that were once used by many of our fathers to make a living and to provide food and clothing for their families. We respect and admire those of our forefathers who lived this way, but we want nothing to do with that kind of life in our modern machine-minded age.

I wonder if our fathers and grandfathers didn't have some things with their hard manual labor [that] we don't have with our labor-saving machinery. Yes, with our power saws and sawmills we prepare lumber faster and better, but are houses better homes? Are we, as fathers, better fathers than our forefathers were? Are we respected and loved as those noble, hardworking fathers were a generation or two ago?

In the early years of our country, a great orator was taken home to spend the night with a humble, hardworking man and his family. The man of the house said to his guest, "Before we retire we always read from the Bible and have prayer." The father, with his family about him, read from the Bible and then prayed for each member of the family, for the church, and for the country, and concluded by praying for their guest and his family.

Telling about it later, [the orator] said, "I have been to Washington and New York, but that night I was at the heart of America's greatness—a father on his knees, praying for his family."

If you are saving some things that remind you of your father or grandfather, don't forget to save his practice of praying for the family. Godly men have passed on to us in this generation a rich legacy. Will we pass on an equally rich legacy to the next generation?

—Harold B. Winn, *Friend to Friend*, p. 55
(Used with permission)

Song: "Faith of Our Fathers"

A Suggested Prayer: May I be faithful in passing the message of your love from my generation to those coming after.

Basket 3
Facing Change

Sandcastles

Bible Reading: Matthew 7:24–29

On a warm summer day on the seashore, one cannot sit long, lazily watching the restless sea, without giving in to the urge to build castles in the sand.

Once started, the imagination has no limits, and before we know it, we have possibly built a castle with balconies, bridges, and walls. And perhaps we decorated with beautiful shells. We feel so protective of our workmanship and guard it from being trampled by children and kicked by adults passing by. But before long, a wave from the incoming tide washes a bit of it away; then, little by little or in one huge swoop, the sandcastle we labored over so meticulously is washed away in the vast ocean waters.

But what do we do if our castles have crumbled?

We must be willing to brave the pain, knowing that God is present, even in the roaring waves that destroyed what we had built together. When the dark waters of life beat upon the relationships that we have built painstakingly and wash them away, we must seek a spot on the shoreline and rebuild. It is imperative that we build our relationships on solid foundation and "stuff" strong enough to withstand life's storms.

We can never build with a guarantee that the waters will never touch us, but our crumbling sandcastles can be a lesson on how to deal with the restless, shifting tides in our lives. Pain and tears are a part of life, but God's spirit will not allow anything to waste. He is just as present in the rolling waves as in the sunshine.

—Frances Pierce, *Refreshings*, pp. 171–172
(Used with permission)

Song: "The Solid Rock"

A Suggested Prayer: Help us not to yield to the temptation of investing our energies and our security in the real estate of sandcastles, attractive though they may appear.

The Revised Plan

Bible Reading: Hebrews 12:1

Rebuilding a home lost in a fire gives an opportunity to improve on what stood before. We begin to imagine changes that will actually make the home more useful. We may also want to include some details that reflect the changes in our family. If the children have left home, we may think smaller. If we have dropped a hobby or added a new career, we may want to redesign the use of a particular room.

Such is the work of mourning [any loss]! We find ourselves in a different world, and we need to rebuild our life with these changes in mind. We've aged. Our family status may be quite different; we may face health challenges. Now that we live in a new world, we need to take time to explore new options.

Redesigning is just good sense but not until after we have had some time to assess our loss and begun to think about the future, rather than focusing on the past. Redesigning will come after we have had time to move away from loss. Then we can begin to see hope in spite of our loss.

To create a new life does not mean finding someone [or something] to fill the hole in our life. That may happen, but it should only happen after we have become whole inside ourselves. Building a new life will bring opportunities and change. Once we have reconciled ourselves with the loss, we are free to explore new options. The new will not seem so frightening when we have made peace with the past.

—Stephen Main, *Fruit*, vol. 49, no. 4, p. 56
(Used with permission)

Song: "What a Friend We Have in Jesus"

A Suggested Prayer: Thank you for showing me my next steps. Help me to move forward with courage and hope.

Retirement

Bible Reading: Psalm 92:12–14

I was in my early forties before the thought of retirement entered my mind. This occurred when a longtime friend offered a few words of advice on his upcoming retirement: "Don't just retire; retire into something." And he wasn't referring to a rocking chair. Psalm 92:12–14 (LB) speaks of how the godly shall flourish, once placed under God's personal care, and that "even in old age they will still produce fruit and be vital and green." In Psalm 90:10 (LB), Moses paints a less rosy picture of our later years: "Seventy years are given us! And some may even live to eighty. But even the best of these years are often emptiness and pain; soon they disappear, and we are gone."

I find retirement to be an extension of my growing-up and working years, still finding the same joys, sorrows and continual change. I have heard that change is the spice of life, and I tend to agree with that statement, until I'm forced out of my own comfort zone. It is also said that from change we either become better or bitter, and since God gave us a free will, we get to choose which it will be. And change does not go away when we enter our "golden years." Actually, it increases, since in addition to generational changes, physical changes related to the aging process must be dealt with.

Looking back on my own life I see nothing but a trail of changes, and after each period of change I see where God, in his infinite mercy, carried me through, making me better (or stronger), not bitter. And change is a must for each and every one of us if we are to stay abreast of the times, learn to relate to the world our children and grandchildren have inherited, and remain their Christian mentor.

—Derl Williams, Wichita, KS

Song: "I Have a Wonderful Peace"

A Suggested Prayer: Father, as the years take their toll on our physical bodies, allow our spirits to continue to "produce fruit and be vital and green."

An Attitude of Gratitude

Bible Reading: II Peter 1:2–9

Happily retired people stay connected to the world. One woman in her nineties, a member of our congregation, was a social activist all her life. She had worked among Native Americans in her early years, and she never lost her drive for peace and justice. In the last year of her life she sometimes called to urge me to write a legislator or attend a rally or donate to a cause. Her life had meaning.

Retired people I admire take care of themselves. They run. They walk. They swim. I'm married to such a person. Nancy insists we eat nutritional meals. Her desire to be fitted with a prosthesis [for her leg] is partly so she can return to her regular exercise program.

I sometimes cheat on my diet because I refuse to let my pancreas totally run my life, but care of the body is a form of stewardship. When old people get together, they often talk about their health—their "organ recital." They'll be able to talk about it longer if they eat, sleep, and exercise well. …

Mostly, a happy retirement is a matter of attitude. Thomas Carlyle wrote: "Our grand business in life is not to see what lies dimly at a distance but to do what lies clearly at hand." People don't get cynical or bitter or grouchy simply because they are old. They probably have had those attitudes for many years. An attitude of gratitude invests life with purpose and joy at age thirty, or earlier, and it continues to do so at age sixty, or longer.

Enthusiasm for life during retirement is a genuine option. I wish it for myself and all others facing retiring years. Years wrinkle the skin, but a lack of enthusiasm for life wrinkles the soul.

—Tom Mullen, *Living Longer*, p. 105
(Used with permission)

Song: "To God Be the Glory"

A Suggested Prayer: We thank you, our Father, for the material comforts we enjoy, but most of all we thank you for seeking and saving us when we were lost and unlovely.

Building Altars

Bible Reading: Genesis 12:4–8; 13:18

Abraham was a traveling man, crossing hundreds of miles on foot during his lifetime. Centralized sanctuaries or temples for worship of Abraham's God did not exist, so he created his own wherever he went.

Travel is a favorite hobby for my wife, Eva, and me. We have been privileged to visit and explore numerous regions at home and abroad. On Sundays we have visited numerous churches and found it refreshing to worship in a manner different from our home church.

We have worshipped with others in majestic cathedrals in Europe and in small Quaker meeting houses. We have worshipped with other believers in the woods at campgrounds. We have worshipped with others aboard ship in the middle of the ocean. Many of these experiences have been quite moving, as we sensed ourselves part of the worldwide fellowship of the saints who worship, love, and trust the same God and Savior as we.

We try to observe the Lord's Day, but it is not always easy—sometimes not even possible—to attend church when traveling. We have become modern-day

Abrahams and have learned to build an altar wherever we are. Sometimes we have lingered in great cathedrals, with eyes lifted to the building's heights and minds lifted to God. Sometimes we have spent quiet time in devotional reading and prayer in our motel room or travel trailer. We have quietly worshipped aboard a tour bus filled with strangers or at tour sites in the Holy Land, which held particular meaning for us.

God's presence has become real to us wherever we have made an altar.

—Leroy Brightup

Song: "Anywhere with Jesus"

A Suggested Prayer: Lord, reign supreme on the altar of my heart that I may worship you wherever I find myself.

Turning Gray and Not Knowing It

Bible Reading: Hosea 7:8–9

Hosea was giving his assessment of what had happened to Israel—they had turned gray without realizing it.

Gray hair is a sign of aging, and I have to acknowledge that balding is such a sign also. The Bible verse noted above gives an example of our tendency to not realize the changes happening to us. It is interesting to look at the wedding anniversary pictures in the newspaper and note the changes that have happened to the couples across the years, changes that surely did not occur all at once.

Change is a fact of life. We are constantly changing. Someone has said that the only constant is change. I was told of a mother who sat in the car, crying while her little son's hair was being cut in the barbershop. When her husband brought the little fellow out to the car, she grabbed her son, kissed him all over his head, and cried and cried. If someone had asked her, "Do you want your little boy to stay a baby forever?" she would have said, "Oh, no, but I'm losing my baby."

Since everything in this life changes, shouldn't we focus on the things of the next life? How sad it is when people reach their senior years, having spent their time and energy only in accumulating this world's goods; as a result they have no treasure in heaven. Jesus said, "Do not store for yourselves treasures on earth, where moth and rust destroy, and where thieves break in and steal. But store up for yourselves treasures in heaven, where moth and rust do not destroy, and where thieves do not break in and steal" (Matt. 6:19–20 [NIV]).

—Francis McKinney, Wichita, KS

Song: "Abide with Me"

A Suggested Prayer: Father, since everything in this world will someday perish, help me to focus on those things that are eternal.

God Lives Here!

Bible Reading: Genesis 28:10–19

We still live in our house and home of over thirty-five years. We now have familiar routines, including when and where we meet God in prayer. We have favorite rooms and chairs for devotional reading and fellowship with God. When these are disrupted, centering and prayer seem more difficult.

But we are giving serious thought to the day we will need to relinquish the responsibilities of home and yard care and upkeep, and move to smaller quarters. Some friends our age have already made choices for relocating.

Many who have been forced to move by reason of age or health have resented the change, feeling alienated from home, family, and church. They have found it difficult to be at peace with their circumstances and with God. My wife tried to help one elderly lady who had to be moved from five different retirement centers because of her dissatisfaction and cantankerous spirit.

In the abovementioned Bible reading, Jacob was on the run far from home. In unfamiliar territory, he turned up a fieldstone in someone's pasture and lay down to sleep. He had a surprising experience.

Waking, he declared, "Surely the Lord is in this place, and I knew it not. This is none other than the house of God." What he had taken to be merely a place to lay his head had become a place of blessing and promise—a sacred sanctuary. This awesome life-shaping experience was so powerful, he marked the spot as a place where God lives, naming it "bethel" (house of God).

However unwelcome a new abode, it can become a place of meeting God. Wherever we re-settle I'm sure it, too, can become a place of worship, a house of God.

—Leroy Brightup

Song: "Anywhere with Jesus"

Prayer Suggestion: Pray for your acquaintances who have had to make adjustments with residing in retirement centers or nursing homes.

Basket 4
Dealing with Loss

Grief Comes

Bible Reading: John 11:1, 17–35

I was saved when I was fourteen years old. I wanted to work for the Lord and prayed he would use me. He said, "Teach my Word." I began teaching at sixteen and taught over seventy years. I am now eighty-nine, and a few months ago I became unable to go to church.

I played the organ for fifty-five years. My husband, Charlie, and I had four children. When Cecil was eleven, Eva eight and a half, Quenton seven, and Jeanette four, they began singing on radio station WMFR in High Point, North Carolina. They were called the Little Hill Quartet and sang every Sunday afternoon at four o'clock for two or three years. I played the organ for them.

When Eva was sixteen, she became ill with a rheumatic heart. About eight years later, she had open-heart surgery. She lived for about two months but passed away on July 27, 1954. I asked the Lord why he did not heal her. He said, "I did. I took her home to heaven, and she will never be sick anymore."

Then in 1983, my grandson Brian was killed in a car wreck in Tyler, Texas, where he lived with his parents. I still grieve for him. My husband passed away ten years ago. I miss him very much, but I know it won't be long until I will go to be with them.

I thank God every day for my three dear children, grandchildren, and great-grandchildren; for my dear pastor and his wife; and for many dear friends who pray for me and visit me. I also thank God every day for his love and help. Praise his name.

—Venia Hill, *Refreshings*, p. 217
(Used with permission)

Song: "It Is Well with My Soul"

Prayer Suggestion: Pray for an acquaintance who is grieving some loss, such as independence, mobility, health, a companion, or other.

For Better or for Worse

Bible Reading: II Timothy 1:5; Job 1:21

As a young woman growing up in a Christian home, I prayed for a godly man to be my husband. In my wedding vows, I promised to love and cherish him "for better or for worse." As a Christian woman, I am also committed to the Lord "for better or for worse." My highest calling was to be a godly wife, godly mother, and godly grandmother, just as my own mother and grandmother were, similar to II Timothy 1:5.

Children are a joy and blessing, but times of dealing with severe family sickness were difficult. There was pneumonia, mononucleosis, a husband with a heart attack and serious blood infection, and—the worst—a thirty-three-year-old daughter diagnosed with terminal cancer. These were not things I had envisioned as a young woman, but God has been faithful in times of "worse."

During the five-plus years our daughter battled cancer, I had the privilege of caring for her and her children, my three grandchildren. I wondered if I would be able to actually assist our daughter and her family, as I'd had migraines and back problems for years. During her care and since, however, the Lord relieved me of these issues, allowing me to do what a mother and grandmother needs to do.

One day, after helping my daughter shower, she had trouble breathing. She said to me, "Mom, you brought me into this world naked. You had to clothe me and feed me, and I will probably leave this world with you doing the same things." With a mother's heavy heart, my response was "Honey, it's my privilege to help you." In the sorrow of our daughter's passing, the Lord comforted us in a time of "worse." I was reminded of Job 1:21 (NIV)—"Naked I came from my mother's womb, and naked I will depart. The Lord gave and the Lord has taken away; may the name of the Lord be praised."

—Eloise Brightup, St. Louis, MO

Song: "Great Is Thy Faithfulness"

A Suggested Prayer: Dear God, you are my "refuge and strength, an ever-present help in trouble" (Psalm 46:1 [NIV]).

Saying Good-Bye

Bible Reading: I Corinthians 15:19–22

My husband, Phil, died in December 1982.

More than five years later, on a First Day (Sunday) after [worship] meeting, I sat visiting with a [Quaker] friend who also was widowed. I asked her if she dreamed about her deceased spouse. When she replied that she seldom did, I told her I still had vivid dreams of mine.

Her response to my statement shocked me, almost as much as if she had slapped me! Yet all she said was "Perhaps he wasn't ready to say good-bye."

Of course he wasn't ready to say good-bye! His death was extremely sudden. We were in a restaurant in Paris, enjoying a wonderful meal and conversation. With no warning and, thankfully, no pain, he was gone. But what shocked me was that in a flash of insight, I realized I was the one who was unwilling to say good-bye!

My friend did not know, and does not know, how she jolted me or how grateful I am to her. With that insight came the courage to say good-bye and to let Phil go, to release him to God. I felt healed of an abiding grief that I seem to have been unable to shed.

I seldom dream of him now, or perhaps I do but the memories are washed away with the morning sun. Yet he is not forgotten and is loved still.

When I said good-bye, I did not separate myself from him, but I did open myself to a new life that has included a new marriage. And best of all, I know that while Phil was not ready to leave us, he is at peace and in a good place.

—B. J. Weatherby, *Refreshings*, p. 215
(Used with permission)

Song: "Beyond the Sunset"

A Suggested Prayer: Thank you, Lord, for the resurrection promise of eternal life with you beyond the grave.

Whispering Hope

Bible Reading: Hebrews 6:16–20

One year ago, my wife, Pattie, passed away. Many have asked me how I am doing, adjusting to life as a widower. The song "Whispering Hope," written by Septimus Winner, has been a lifelong inspiration to me, and a phrase in the chorus expresses what has transpired in me this past year as a result of that hope: "making my heart in its sorrow rejoice."

To me, the "whispering hope" is the still small voice of God. I need not tell you that the sorrow is real. Indeed, I have grieved and still do grieve the loss. Two made one in Christ produced a most joyful companionship and a life-enhancing intimacy. This loss is the source of my deepest grief, as well as my greatest joy and reason for celebration. In spite of Pattie's death, there is still a sense of presence in the memory of her spirit and life. Those same memories offer a firm footing for the ongoing journey of life.

I live a fairly structured life, and life continues—except now without the caregiving responsibilities and without the companionship on which I thrived. I am certainly blessed through the wonderful support of family, my church, the Friends University constituency, and so many more from the community at large.

Encouragement from this support network has helped make my heart, in its sorrow, rejoice.

With God's guidance, mine shall be a "good" grief that refuses to live in the past, while celebrating past blessing—one that will enable embracing and enjoying life and anticipating a promising future; one that is a stepping stone rather than a stumbling block.

—Duane M. Hansen, Wichita, KS

Song: "Whispering Hope"

A Suggested Prayer: Lord, you said, "I will not leave you comfortless: I will come to you" (John 14:18 [KJV]). Thanks for the hope you give, enabling celebration in sorrow and grief.

Grief as Gift

Bible Reading: John 14:18

The loss of a treasure evokes grief—no treasure, no loss, no grief. The loss of a God-given treasure is the reason we grieve. Even so, grief is not unique to seniors, although it may come with greater frequency to them.

Everyone grieves uniquely—some more cognitively, others more emotionally. Some grief is handled in stride; other grief is life-changing.

Grieving is not an easy process—from treasure, to loss, to grief, to recovery, and then living happily ever after. It was in retrospect that I realized when my grieving began.

We learned of Pattie's breast cancer in December 1999. In 2000 she had chemotherapy, a lumpectomy, and radiation. She lost about thirty pounds and experienced many treatment side effects. She returned to work in November 2000 and worked until the cancer returned in her lung and sternum in October 2005. Still, we experienced three more wonderful years of companionship and joy.

With the December 2007 brain cancer diagnosis, a major shifting of responsibilities began. (Although I was unaware at the time, my grieving process began in earnest *then*.) Along with caregiving, I became chief cook, merry dude housekeeper, and laundryman. Painful as these changes were, they helped moderate my grief after her death and still even now.

Grief is part of life, so grieve as you must. Remember that your grief does not justify always feeling sad, but the loss of a God-given treasure is reason to grieve. So truthfully, grieving is also a God-given gift!

—Duane M. Hansen, Wichita, KS

Song: "In the Garden"

A Suggested Prayer: Dear Lord, help me to treasure your blessings that make my loss a thing to grieve. Thanks for your love and nearness in my journey back to celebration.

Blessing from a Place of Sadness

Bible Reading: Matthew 5:4

Jesus said, "Blessed are those who mourn, for they shall be comforted" (NASB). We usually interpret this as a call for a humble spirit, but I want to use Jesus's words to talk about the actual mourning experience. (I am a retired pastor and work in a funeral home part-time.) Mourning can be emotionally exhausting, and it is something we naturally avoid.

Mourning happens with any great loss: a death, a divorce, the loss of a job, or separation from someone important to us. Years ago, when a family lost a loved one, the widow would dress in mourning clothes for a month or six weeks, and we would mark the house with a wreath to tell everyone that the home was going through a special loss. Now, our neighbor may be mourning, and we know nothing about the experience. Some choose to do nothing in a public way to acknowledge the loss, and the journey through the grief process can be a very lonely experience. Perhaps our losses, more than our successes, are what truly define our character.

Out of the saddest times in our life, we learn to be compassionate. Jesus would not have had an authentic human experience if he had been protected from suffering and pain. While we can read through these lessons in a [short time], it will usually take years for us to walk down the path of mourning.

—Stephen Main, *Fruit*, vol. 49, no. 4, p. 51
(Used with permission)

Song: "When We All Get to Heaven"

A Suggested Prayer: Lord, help us to trust you, even when we feel lonely and wonder why we have to go through a time of sorrow.

Alone with Jesus

Bible Reading: Genesis 23:2

Mourning is doing something about a loss that is so important to us. We take time out of our regular schedule to walk alone through the memories to a place where we can build a new life. For most of us, mourning is something we do with family and friends. Our loss is made more real when we see the body, move our things out of the office, or pack up the car and drive to our new home. These moments of "reality" may bring tears to our eyes. We may feel anger because we have been cheated somehow. We may feel very alone and afraid of the future. It is here that we greatly need the companionship of family and friends.

In dealing with our loss, one of the things we do is look for the lost item or person. We spend time looking for the lost in hope [that] we can restore our life to what has been normal. We may actually have moments when we see the loved one in a group somewhere, only to later discover we were wrong. Dreams are a common way we subconsciously try to bring the lost one back into our life.

We use the phrase, "We lost Uncle John," to define a very real part of our grief. Defining what we have lost is an important part of the healing process.

—Stephen Main, *Fruit*, vol. 49, no. 4, p. 52
(Used with permission)

Song: "We'll Understand It Better, By and By"

A Suggested Prayer: Lord, this is a very difficult time for me. Please fill the ache in my heart with your presence. I do trust you, even though my loss hurts so much.

Sorrow without Despair

Bible Reading: Job 1:20–22

Our loss will be expressed in a way that is very personal for us. For some, a community event allows interaction with family and friends. Others may need solitude, and their mourning is done in private moments. Some may need a walk down a familiar path or quiet hours sitting in the backyard. Looking through old photo albums may be helpful to identify special moments. During the process of mourning we again touch the deep sadness of our loss, and then we move to a sense of comfort. As we go through these periods, they become less intense, and we begin to see with gratitude what a privilege it was to have had this person in our life.

Our loss is directly related to the wonderful things we enjoyed because of this person or opportunity. To be separated from the comfort and security of family and friends may be the price one pays to move to a new job. I like to think of holding the sadness in my hands, like one would hold a treasured object to admire its beauty. Holding my loss, feeling the sadness, and then setting it down to be picked up at another time can be very helpful.

As the focus moves from the loss to an awareness of how blessed we were to have a particular person in our life, we build steps of strength back into our life. It is a short step toward health when instead of the loss, we see how blessed we were by that individual.

—Stephen Main, *Fruit*, vol. 49, no. 4, p. 53
(Used with permission)

Song: "Does Jesus Care?"

A Suggested Prayer: Thank you, Lord, for giving me a life that included _____. My life seems so broken now. Help me follow you through this rebuilding time.

Basket 5
Utilizing Time

It's about Time

Bible Reading: Ephesians 5:15–16; I Peter 1:17

A few years ago, while visiting our daughter and her family in Washington State, some of us went through Ape Cave. Eventually, we reached a spot where assistance was very helpful in climbing to a higher level. Fortunately, there were two park rangers there to give help. I heard one of the rangers comment, "We were told to watch for an elderly man coming through." I knew he meant me. Later, I remarked on his statement and jokingly said, "I started looking for that elderly man but never did see him."

There was a time when the "elderly" were those older folks. Now, it is *us*. Now, there may be some loss of eyesight, some difficulty in hearing, some decline in energy and vitality, and some loss of elasticity of muscles. How shall we respond to these changes?

We can lament, or we can make the rest of our years the best of our years.

Each of us has a time account that we should use wisely. President Franklin Roosevelt visited Justice Oliver Wendell Holmes and found him, at the age of ninety-two, reading Plato. When the president asked why, Holmes's answer was simply, "To improve my mind." He was still trying to use his time account wisely.

—Francis McKinney, Wichita, KS

Song: "I'll Live for Him"

A Suggested Prayer: Thank you, Father, for the minutes you give us. May we truly live them for your glory.

Anticipating Retirement

Bible Reading: I Corinthians 10:23–31

Retirement often disappoints. Some work harder at loafing than they used to loaf at working. Spouses discover that they had married for better or worse but not for lunch. Retired people have to drink coffee on their own time. When the moment finally arrives when people can do anything they wish, they wish they could do something else.

At this writing I am almost but not yet retired. ... What worries this product of the Puritan work ethic is the open-endedness of retirement. As an observer of retired people, it seems they never do all the stuff they intended to do when they didn't have the time.

Wasting time was a cardinal sin in my boyhood home, and I carry those feelings to this day. I understand that time does not always have to be productive in the traditional sense. Reading books, enjoying music, playing with grandchildren, and watching sunsets are worth doing. Robert Fulghum reminds us that almost no one ever wishes he or she had spent more time at the office. Experiencing life is its own excuse for being.

But simply filling time, I've been taught, is wasteful. Before any of us retire, we should be required to sit at home for a week and watch daytime television. This is a foolproof recipe for wasting time. The fear I bring, as retirement draws near, is that I will wake up in the morning with nothing useful to do and go to bed at night with it still to be done.

Those who model a happy retirement meet two criteria: they have something to live on and much to live for.

—Tom Mullen, *Living Longer*, p. 104
(Used with permission)

Song: "God of Our Life, through All the Circling Years"

A Suggested Prayer: Help us to focus our minds and our efforts on those things that are beneficial, enriching, and uplifting.

Volunteering

Bible Reading: Colossians 3:17

After retiring from Boeing Airplane Company, I felt a desire to be associated with a Christian organization. Through an ad in a church newsletter, the Lord led me to an organization that ministers to the needs of the poor in our city. It was here that I was to meet my husband, who also had a heart for ministry and a desire to serve the Lord in his senior years. Little did we realize what the Lord had in store for us.

We purchased a motor home to travel and see the United States. The Lord fine-tuned that desire through people and circumstances (our steps are ordered of the Lord—Psalm 37:23). He led us to an organization called Mobile Missionary Assistance Program (MMAP) that has projects for volunteers all over the United States. In serving with MMAP we have traveled the United States and helped Christian organizations along the way. Each project lasts three weeks, and we meet for devotions five days a week at 7:30 a.m. All individuals are retired, and most of us have some physical handicaps—bad knee, bad back, bad shoulder, heart problems, etc. ("We have this treasure in an earthen vessel that the excellency of the power may be of God and not of us" [II Cor. 4:7]). As the men go to work, it reminds me of the song from *Snow White and the Seven Dwarfs*: "Hi-ho, it's off to work we go." I find it comical, as most are limping, favoring some part of their anatomy.

Truly, it is in giving that we are blessed!

—Velda Kuhns, Wichita, KS

Song: "Take My Life"

A Suggested Prayer: Make me an instrument of your love, mercy, and grace today.

Ministers

Bible Reading: Matthew 25:31–40

"For I was an hungred and ye gave me meat, I was thirsty and ye gave me drink, I was a stranger and ye took me in" (Matthew 25:35).

Jesus was a perfect man, both human and divine. When his work on earth was finished, he admonished his disciples to continue preaching the Gospel to the ends of the earth.

Our ministers are still proclaiming the good news to a needy world. Do we support and encourage them as we should?

One of my personal ministries of service is to visit the sick, shut-ins, and discouraged and lonely people. I have prepared meals and entertained many pastors, evangelists, and Christian workers through the years. Now, at eighty-five, to fellowship and eat with God's servants around the table has been and continues to be a joy and one of the highlights of my life.

I encourage families to invite their pastor into their home for a meal and fellowship. Ministers are people like you and me. They enjoy good home-cooked food also. You will receive a blessing and find it rewarding.

We should thank God continually for our pastors, teachers, leaders, and parents who point out the shortcomings of our society and nation and warn of the inevitable.

A challenge of today is to walk through new doors, seize new opportunities, to defeat the evil so prevalent in our world of unrest and confusion. May God richly bless our ministers and leaders who labor hard and long to save our country.

II Timothy 2:15: "Study to show thyself approved unto God; a workman that needeth not to be ashamed."

—Bonnie Hinshaw, *Refreshings*, p. 141
(Used with permission)

Song: "I Love to Tell the Story"

Prayer Suggestion: Pray for your pastor or chaplain and for any you know who are involved in inner-city mission work.

The Ministry of Prayer

Bible Reading: Colossians 4:2–4; II Thessalonians 3:1–4

As old age creeps up, there are changes in the ministry roles to which God calls his servants. For me, God had always opened leadership positions: chairing committees, serving as president of women's groups, public speaking, teaching Sunday school. One of my greatest joys was music: directing or accompanying choirs, singing solos, or singing in ensembles.

With retirement came fewer leadership responsibilities, and with last year's serious illness, a complete halt to any such ministry. Having to spend hours in bed meant lying awake at night. It was then that God became very near and personal, impressing on me the names and faces of those for whom I should pray.

Taking intercession seriously, my husband and I now spend lengthy time each morning praying "around the world." Not only do we intercede for Friends pastors and missionaries but for people groups and those who minister to them that we know only through media channels.

An Evangelical Friends Missions leader in Nepal, while on furlough, spoke at Hayden Lake Church.

He mentioned a "blind spot" he has noticed in the American church. When quizzed about what the blind spot might be, his answer was, "Prayerlessness. The American church has lost the discipline of prayer." As he visited churches, he urged the congregations not only to pray but also to fast. Nepalese Christians set the example in this practice and are seeing many answers to prayer, with hundreds turning from Hinduism, Buddhism, and Islamic beliefs to receive Jesus Christ.

—Marjorie Crisman, *Fruit*, vol. 49, no. 3, p. 85
(Used with permission)

Song: "'Tis the Blessed Hour of Prayer"

A Suggested Prayer: "Our Father which art in heaven, Hallowed be thy name. Thy kingdom come. Thy will be done in earth, as it is in heaven. Give us this day our daily bread. And forgive us our debts, as we forgive our debtors. And lead us not into temptation, but deliver us from evil: For thine is the kingdom, and the power and the glory, forever. Amen" (Matthew 6:9–13).

Blessings Bring Responsibility

Bible Reading: Titus 2:7–8

As I write this in 2003, which is ninety years after 1913 when I was born, I see many changes. But it isn't as if I have been asleep for ninety years! I have been aware of the changes and have experienced both the good and the bad that goes with them. There has been a big change in lifestyle in many homes. My parents were not wealthy by any measure of earthly things, yet our lives were happy and comfortable, and generally rural life then was much more desirable than a great deal of city living now. Most women were homemakers and had pride in their home, humble or lavish. We were used to kerosene lamps and outside toilets, but there was style, dignity, and beauty in everyday living and manners, home furnishings, table manners, and conversation.

Of course, much has changed since I was a child! Much has changed in every century, even in every generation. But much has *not* changed. We still have problems. A war touched nearly every generation in some way.

The Bible records many, many conflicts. Man is sinful, and sinful people do sinful things that have to be stopped. We never learn! We can get very discouraged unless we remember that God knows all about our problems. He has a plan for us. We can put up with this world, helping to keep virtue and goodness alive by accepting God and his plan for our salvation through Jesus Christ.

All of us can do our part by praying for the world, by giving gifts for the teaching of God's Word and his plan for life and eternity, and by being an example of a godly life. We can help by giving our talents, time, and money for the spiritually and physically needy (at home and around the world). Our blessings received bring a responsibility to share them!

—Faye McCoy, *One Generation*, p. 64
(Used with permission)

Song: "Make Me a Blessing"

A Suggested Prayer: It is my high privilege to be your servant in response to your love. May I be faithful until the end.

A Right Time for Everything

Bible Reading: Ecclesiastes 3:1–11; 9:10

I anticipated retirement as a time of quiet relaxation, traveling with my husband, Gary, and "thumb-twiddling," but God soon made it evident that he had other plans for me. Certainly, my retirement expectations have greatly differed from my realities.

First came the opportunity to be the presiding clerk of University Friends Meeting. This has been a growing, stretching experience for me, demanding wisdom and strength far beyond my own. I didn't expect or desire to be in a position of leadership at this time in my life. I was ready to hand off the torch to younger folks. So I have had to depend on the Lord to use my gifts as he wills, when he wills.

Next, the Lord brought the chance for Gary and me to be grandparents—first to Macie, now four, and then to Riley, ten weeks old. We're blessed to have lived to enjoy the grandchildren we never expected. What a joy to care for them and to nurture them in the love of Jesus. True, it has diminished leisure time and spur-of-the-moment activities. In exchange, we experience anew the joy and wonder with which children approach life.

In my ear, I hear the voice of my mother, Esther Choate, reminding me, "Whatsoever thy hand findeth to do, do it with thy might" (Ecclesiastes 9:10). That is what retirement has offered—lots of unexpected "whatsoevers," and I am attempting to do them faithfully, in the strength and joy of the Lord.

—Ann Fuqua, Wichita, KS

Editors' note: Ann died in a car accident while this book was in progress.

Song: "Make Me a Blessing"

A Suggested Prayer: In whatever you bring to me for my hand to do, Lord, please make me a blessing today.

Basket 6
Beginning Anew

A Forgiven Past

Bible Reading: Philippians 3:12–16

Today, many place great emphasis on memory and memory training. But just as important as good memory is good forgettery! We're not to forget all the past but only what keeps us from living fully in the present. Forget the past that paralyzes the present. This we can do by God's grace. The apostle Paul said in [the abovementioned Bible] reading, "Forgetting what is behind …" (NIV).

In one of her poems, Louisa Fletcher Tarkington expresses the longing for a place where all of our mistakes and heartaches could be dropped and abandoned forever. This is made possible through Calvary. The atonement of Christ has made us righteous; that is, right with God. "It's what God does with your life as he sets it right …" (Romans 14:17 [The Message]). We are no longer separated in our relationships; we're right with God, self, and others.

Every Christian occasionally needs to ask, "Am I presently bound by anything in the past that keeps me from being victorious in the present?" If the answer is yes, confess your old wounds and let Christ dress them. Take the hurts, the disappointments, the shattered hopes and dreams, and let him set your life right. How wonderful to have a forgiven past!

—Robert A. Crandall, *Fruit,* vol. 40, no. 3, p. 109
(Used with permission)

Song: "Love Divine, All Loves Excelling"

A Suggested Prayer: Thank you, Lord, for forgiving the past to give me freedom in the present.

Have You Seen Jesus?

Bible Reading: Luke 19:1–9

We read that Zacchaeus, a rich tax collector who had cheated many people, was not only small in stature but was curious. When Jesus was passing through Jericho, Zacchaeus found only one way to solve his curiosity—he climbed up in a sycamore tree so that he could see Jesus. Jesus saw Zacchaeus and told him to come down, which he immediately did. The Bible says that Zacchaeus already knew he had wronged the taxpayers, and he repented and accepted Jesus that very day.

We are often convicted of our wrongdoing but are not willing to repent. We need to come down from our "tree" of self-confidence, greed, pride, self-ambition, rebellion, and anything that is keeping us from fellowship with Jesus. Zacchaeus may have gotten by with his sins until he met Jesus, but his willingness to ask for forgiveness made him a new man.

In what type of "tree" are you hiding? Jesus has a new life for you if you are willing to say, "God, be merciful to me, a sinner."

—Barbara Smitherman, Haviland, KS

Song: "Thank You, Lord, for Saving My Soul"

A Suggested Prayer: Speak to me today in my particular need and help me be willing to give myself totally to you. Thank you for your love in spite of our frequent neglect to call on you. Thank you for salvation that brings freedom.

Weeds

Bible Reading: Ephesians 4:29–32

Ralph Wolford has been crippled with arthritis or rheumatism for several years and walks with a cane. He likes to see a garden grow and does a good job at raising vegetables. When I stopped in to see Ralph and Laura, his wife, there was Ralph, working his garden. He was not hoeing it like most of us would; he was down on his knees looking for weeds and cultivating the ground around the tomatoes. The garden was as weedless as you would find anywhere.

In his condition most people would say that they couldn't have a garden. However, Ralph goes to his knees in planting and working his garden and has a much better garden than most people have who don't have any trouble with rheumatism.

As Ralph could never get the weeds out of his garden without knee work, so there are some weeds which come up in the garden of our hearts, which none of us can get out unless we get on our knees and do some praying. There are the weeds of bitterness, hatred, revenge, jealousy, and malice, which will grow like quack grass in a human heart unless they are pulled up and destroyed.

Turning to God in prayer about one's needs means that God helps one to get his heart free from these choking, strength-taking enemies of the soul and life. Many a person is like a weed-filled garden. They started out so promising, but the weeds of sin took over, and now they are unproductive, weak, defeated, and despondent. All they need is to get on their knees, seek God's help, tear out these weeds, and hand them to God, and God will take them clear off the premises and destroy them. This doesn't mean one just prays once and that is all. No, one must do a lot of knee work as long as there is the garden of the heart [that] will last until death comes.

—Harold B. Winn, *Friend to Friend*, p. 34
(Used with permission)

Song: "Cleanse Me"

Prayer Suggestion: Try Ralph's knee-work method for some choking weeds you sense in your heart.

Lessons from the Compost Pile

Bible Reading: Philippians 1:3–6

A short article by Judy Cannato in an issue of the Christian journal *Weavings* caught my imagination. The title was "The Compost Pile," and she set out to challenge the reader to be open to the need for transformation in order to make our personalities more usable in the kingdom.

Composting is a way of using our refuse to make rich fertilizer to help our new plants grow and flourish, but the elements of the compost pile must be in balance or refuse just remains stinky garbage. It needs some dead leaves and grass clippings (unkind words, inconsiderate actions?); scraps of fruit and vegetables (a compassionate heart, a thirst for God?); moisture (tears of regret or pain?); air from being stirred up; and biodegraders such as earthworms to break it down (perhaps other people in one's life?).

So we bring the compostable part of ourselves—the unlovely, the possibilities, the hope—and we yield all of it to God, and we wait for him to bring about transformation.

—Eva Brightup

Song: "Change Me, O God"

A Suggested Prayer: May I be open to change, Lord, in order that I may be more like you.

On Loving God

Bible Reading: Mark 12:28–30

Many of us have grown up with a rather austere view of God. Although familiar from childhood with John 3:16 and the Bible reading from Mark, above, in some way the idea of my *loving* God never gripped me. The idea of a caring attachment did not surface. Believe in him, yes. Believe correctly about him, yes. Fear him, yes. Obey him, yes. Thank him, yes. But *love* him?

In reading Dallas Willard's book *The Divine Conspiracy*, I was arrested by the idea that the first objective in a curriculum for Christlikeness is to let one's mind become enthralled with love for God. My mind was not so enthralled. I did not delight in *loving* God. Where had I missed the message? How had love of God failed to blossom in my mind and heart?

Willard said the first step in learning to love God is to reflect on all he has done for us. As I dwelt on this idea, biblical passages began to flood my mind: "We love because he first loved us" (I John 4:19 [NRSV]); "God, being rich in mercy, because of his great love with which he loved us, even when we were dead in our transgressions ..." (Eph. 2:4–5 [NASB]); "God put his love on the line for us when we were of no use whatever to him" (Rom. 5:8 [The Message]).

My heart warmed. In light of all the ways he has shown his love, I was gripped by the idea that my only proper response was to love him in return. In *Embracing the Love of God*, James Bryan Smith teaches us that "God is madly in love with us." And I have begun to believe it, and that he treasures our love in return.

Now in my seventies, I have discovered not just a master/servant relationship but an adventurous love relationship, delighting in the things he cares about.

—Leroy Brightup

Song: "More Love to Thee, O Christ"

A Suggested Prayer: May my love for you grow deeper and deeper each day as I meditate on your unending love for me.

Later in Life

Bible Reading: Matthew 11:28–30

At fifty-seven years old, I felt anchorless, with no one steering the ship. My children were raised, leaving my goals and ambitions seemingly dissipated like a puff of smoke. Spending many solitary hours in self-examination, my thoughts ran in circles, always returning to an open-ended conclusion: there had to be something more than this, but what? I didn't know my son [Jim] was grappling with similar thoughts.

One evening, Jim came through the doorway. "Mom," he said, "I was watching Billy Graham's crusade on TV, and when he gave the call for anyone wanting to receive Jesus Christ as Savior, I went up to the TV set and knelt down." He gulped. "I've been saved, Mom!" Jim began avidly reading his Bible as I listened to what he was learning.

Then I spent a night at the home of an old friend, a wonderful Christian woman. I went to bed, pondering unanswered questions mingled with feelings of heaviness and despair.

The next morning, with the early sunlight, disturbing thoughts crowded into my mind. I saw my life as a hopeless tangle of circles, going nowhere. Despite my lifelong belief in God, I had never been saved. At that moment, I pleaded for the Lord Jesus to come into my life.

Since, Jim and I have been delighted with our lives. We continue dealing with problems and concerns, but see them from God's point of view and handle them accordingly. We experience peace where it had never been before.

About five years ago, my daughter Hilary became a born-again Christian, an answer to our many prayers. I am pleased my granddaughter, Terri, her husband, Scott, and their four children are also Christians!

—Ruth E. Furr, *Stewardship*, vol. 43, no. 3, pp. 11–12
(Used with permission)

Song: "Since Jesus Came into My Heart"

A Suggested Prayer: Thank you, God, for giving purpose to our lives when we put them in your hands.

My Wealth

Bible Reading: Matthew 6:19–21

After I began to receive Social Security at age sixty-five, I worked full time until I was seventy years old; then twenty hours a week until I was eighty. The government programs paid minimum wage, but work was plentiful, usually in a pleasant environment. Approaching my eightieth birthday, I terminated my employment.

My son Jim and I live together, so his modest income added to my Social Security check usually pays our expenses. We lean on the Lord to provide for our needs when we can't.

Last year, with the economic recession closing in, the state of our finances was making me uncomfortable. I knew the Lord was in control and could provide for our needs if necessary, yet I wondered if we were overlooking some remedies.

I made an appointment with my Mennonite Mutual Aid counselor to discuss my options. His conclusion: we were handling the situation reasonably well. It was encouraging to know we were on the right track

The dismaying conditions prevailing around the world concern us but aren't overly frightening. First, Jim and I, having already survived many economic perils, have learned to choose between needs and wants. Secondly, we stand firm in the knowledge that God is in total control ... and it can't get any better than that!

I anticipate attaining my ninetieth birthday in reasonably good health this coming Christmas Day. Although I have no worldly riches to show for my years, I am thankful for the abundant spiritual riches I do have. Every member of my small but beloved family is a Christian!

—Ruth E. Furr, *Stewardship*, vol. 43, no. 3, pp. 12–13
(Used with permission)

Song: "Jesus Is All the World to Me"

Prayer Suggestion: Ask God if there is a person or a charity in economic difficulty to whom you should make a financial gift.

Basket 7
Experiencing Need

God Knows Our Needs

Bible Reading: Matthew 6:7–13

Recently I saw several milk bottles in an antique shop. It came to me with a jolt that these very familiar utensils of my early life have now become a curiosity. I remember so well, walking out on a January morning to see an icy column of frozen milk pushing a paper stopper high out of the neck of one of these bottles. What a joy it was to see the half-pint bottles come in from the dairy. We knew this meant strawberry shortcake and whipped cream.

My encounter with the "antique" bottles reminded me of a true story. Back in the golden days of these rare containers, each member of a family shared the home chores. One cold winter night after supper, sisters were washing dishes as the little brother gathered up the empty milk bottles to put out on the front steps for the milkman. The little fellow opened the front door, took a brief look outside, stepped back in, and said to his dad, "It's too dark a night to be out without a father."

How often do we feel this way? There are far too many overwhelming situations for any of us to face alone. The light in these dark nights is that we are not without a father. We have the blessed assurance that underneath are the everlasting arms.

At any age or in any age, God is always present and knows our needs, even before we ask for help. What a freeing realization!

—Marietta M. Forlaw, *Refreshings*, pp. 167–168
(Used with permission)

Song: "God Will Take Care of You"

Prayer Suggestion: Pray for someone of your acquaintance who seems to be trying to live without the assistance of our heavenly Father's comfort and guidance.

Fears

Bible Reading: Isaiah 41:10–14

I was making a pastoral call one afternoon when six or seven coon dogs came running and barking to greet me. I tried to act brave and be friendly, but those dogs kept barking and snipping at me. All the time, I was working my way over to a tractor. When I got there, I jumped up on it. They acted like they had the prize "coon" up a tree. I made up my mind that I was going to stay right there until someone came. Fortunately, the man was home, and he came out and called his dogs off and welcomed me into his home with apologies.

Every person, we are told, has some fear or phobia. It may be only one, but if we have just one, it is tormenting. It may be the fear of being alone or of darkness, or of mice or of heights or of some other ridiculous thing. A fear has the power to tie one's stomach up in knots. It makes a person want to run. Science has discovered that fears are like certain watches; they are self-winding. Running from a fear keeps the fear active.

The Bible tells us how to overcome some fears. It teaches, in many places, that the basic answer to our spiritual fears, such as the fear of death, the fear of meeting God, and the fear of a terrible tragedy, is to know that we are right with God. The confident presence of God with us is the only guarantee for freedom from these tormenting fears.

God said this to a man many years ago, and he will make it personal to you and to me if we will let him: "Fear thou not; for I am with thee: be not dismayed; for I am thy God. I will strengthen thee; yea, I will help thee" (Isaiah 41:10).

—Harold B. Winn, *Friend to Friend*, p. 37
(Used with permission)

Song: "Jesus, Savior, Pilot Me"

A Suggested Prayer: I offer up my fear today and ask that it be replaced with a calm trust in my Savior and Lord.

The Need for New Friends in Our Later Years

Bible Reading; John 15:14–17

I've been rereading *Learn to Grow Old* by Paul Tournier, the Swiss psychologist. He points out that if we do not continue making friends during our later years, we may soon find ourselves without any, because former friends may move away or die.

If we moved, we would need to seek new friends. Friendships, however, are not born whole. Friendships start from a base of recognized but scattered bits of commonality and often take years to bloom and flower. Developing friendships calls for investment of time and energy. We still have both. Ten years from now, it might be considerably more difficult, so wouldn't we be wise in moving now?

At the same time, one of the most wrenching aspects of moving will be living at a distance from our old friends and visiting them only occasionally. Can we hope to develop the same degree of intimacy and feel the same sense of security with new friends? Our new friends gained in our later years will be known to us only in their aging; we'll never know what kind of persons they were in their prime.

How can we know the answer? I'm beginning to sense that, for various reasons, the aging person experiences loneliness. Perhaps this will motivate me all the more to concentrate on developing a deeper intimacy with Jesus.

—Mildred Tengbom, *Moving*, p. 56
(Used with permission)

Song: "No One Ever Cared for Me Like Jesus"

A Suggested Prayer: No friend is truer than you, Lord. Remind us of your nearness in our moments of loneliness.

The Voice of the Shepherd

Bible Reading: John 10:1–6

A few years ago, my husband and I had the privilege of visiting Israel and Jordan. One evening, near sunset, we were traveling down a lonely stretch of road, surrounded on all sides by nothing but barren sand and an occasional Bedouin tent. Suddenly, off to the right, our guide pointed out a lone shepherd leading his flock home for the night. The driver stopped our bus, and we watched as shepherd and sheep slowly made their way back to their tent shelter. The sheep were neither running ahead nor lagging behind, and I noticed they were not scrawny, undernourished animals. Apparently, the shepherd knew something I could not see—the location of food and water—and the sheep trusted the shepherd for the provision.

More recently, a friend told me of seeing the use of common pastures for sheepherding in Wales. I wondered how the shepherds ever got their flocks divided up when evening came. My mind went to the narrative of the Good Shepherd, recorded in John 10, in which Jesus says the Good Shepherd's sheep follow him "because they know his voice." In the previous verse, he says, "He calls his own sheep by name and leads them out" (NIV).

What a picture of how our relationship should be with the Shepherd of our souls! But first, we must learn to recognize the voice of the Shepherd, and we do that by spending time with him and becoming familiar with his spirit and actions, often from the explicit statements of Jesus himself.

—Eva Brightup

Song: "Savior, Like a Shepherd Lead Us"

A Suggested Prayer: We long to know your voice. Teach us to recognize it and follow.

The Waste of Worry

Bible Reading: Luke 12:22–31

I suspect [Luke 12:22–31] speaks to many of us. It does to me. A recently retired physician told me that 85 percent of the patients he saw in his family practice came because of worry. Worry wreaks havoc on the mind and body. We can legitimately be aware of our needs, but they're not to be the focus of life. Jesus says we're not to worry about food or clothes. But we fret over other things as well. Many people are caught up in worrying about their children, their work, their finances, and even their aches and pains. The cares of life become the overriding concern.

While I was writing these devotionals, I began to worry over something that had happened. As I lay awake one night I saw an image of Jesus putting out a "No Trespassing" sign on my worry, as if he were saying, "This is for me to handle, not you. Don't go there!" With that, I fell peacefully asleep.

When we focus on what we don't have rather than on what we do have, we are being ungrateful. Worrying also assumes we can care for the situation rather than trust God to provide the answer. Worry is wasteful; it accomplishes nothing. Let God have your concerns; take your burdens to the Lord and leave them there.

—Robert A. Crandall, *Fruit*, vol. 40, no. 3, p. 106
(Used with permission)

Song: "My Hope Is in the Lord"

A Suggested Prayer: Dear Lord, forgive my lack of trust in your ability to provide for my needs. Help me to live in total reliance upon you.

The Older I Get, the More Money I Need

Bible Reading: Isaiah 46:4

It seems that as we age our income decreases, but our expenses increase. We need glasses, hearing aids, special foods, medications, canes, walkers, and visits to doctors. We need special shoes and warmer clothing and houses. With smaller income, how can we afford these things we need because of our lessening abilities?

I am thankful for senior citizen discounts, for insurance and Social Security. Even so, it is sometimes difficult. However, I must acknowledge that what I have really needed, the Lord has supplied in some way. He is able, and he has promised. He didn't say he would provide all our needs up until age sixty (or into our nineties, where I am), and then we are on our own. No, in Isaiah he says he will carry us, even when we are old and gray (or white).

When my husband died recently, my income was reduced, but expenses have been nearly as much as before. Then I began needing special medical treatments and expensive medicines, plus incurring additional transportation costs. I had made commitments to give my tithe to several Christian organizations. Should I cut down on my giving now? I decided to continue my gifts and trust the Lord to supply my needs. This is working just fine. He is providing, month by month.

Psalm 92:13–14 gives me hope that I can still be of some use to God and others, even in old age. "Those that be planted in the house of the Lord shall flourish. ... They shall still bring forth fruit in old age."

—Leigh Parcel, Wichita, KS

Song: "God Will Take Care of You"

A Suggested Prayer: Dear Lord, please help us to really trust you to take care of us, even in old age.

Basket 8
Trusting God

Forever Faithful and True

Bible Reading: Joshua 1:5

Growing up in a Christian home, I learned from the time I was a child about God—who he is and that he is always there, always loving and caring. As I grow older, I find this is still a great comfort to me, and his promises become more real and precious to me. Throughout our marriage, in addition to an abundance of joyous occasions, my husband and I also have known heartache, physical problems, and times of distress and grief. God has proven himself to be faithful in every instance.

When our oldest son left for South America right after high school graduation to serve with Wycliffe Bible Translators for a year, I missed him so much, as well as being concerned for him in a far away place. God gave me the promise found in Philippians 4:19 (NIV): "And my God will meet all your needs according to his glorious riches in Christ Jesus." I trusted him to meet *all* our needs and of course, he did and continues to do so.

I find that as my body ages, at times things happen that I didn't even know existed, and I don't know what the future may bring; still, I can lean on him who says, "I will never leave you nor forsake you." I pray I will always know this, no matter the circumstances. He is faithful!

—Naomi Weinacht, Nampa, ID

Song: "Great Is Thy Faithfulness"

A Suggested Prayer: Lord, thank you for being my Savior and friend and for your guidance and love throughout my life.

God Is Good

Bible Reading: Psalm 136

God has given me a good life and the health and faculties to enjoy it. I am ninety-eight years of age and live in the nursing facility of a retirement center. Most of my working years were spent as an English teacher at Friends University in Wichita, Kansas. Unmarried, I had the freedom to travel with student groups and to accept a variety of assignments beyond the classroom. Serving for a time as a "mother" to the girls in the dorm provided some challenging and frightening moments. That was a learning experience! But God provided grace, and I survived.

When the university president and his wife were to be in Africa for several weeks, I was asked to house-sit for them. Although Ann had oriented me to the house, little did I realize that guest hospitality came with the job. When visitors to campus started arriving unannounced, I was overwhelmed. I did not consider myself a cook, and after a few attempts simply told guests that their meals could be taken at the school cafeteria. Again, God saw me through that experience.

My life is full of people I have loved and remembered. I give thanks for the gift of learning and sharing life with loving people. I give thanks for a clear mind and the ability to remember. Some former students whom I had not seen in decades visited me recently. To their surprise and mine, I was able to recognize each and call them by name. I give thanks for reasonably good health. I get out frequently and have the eyesight to enjoy the changing colors of nature. God is good.

—Essie Platt, Wichita, KS

Editors' note: Essie's devotional was summarized from seven pages of material, beautifully written in longhand and clearly legible. She died quietly a few weeks after submitting this material.

Song: "Love Divine, All Loves Excelling"

A Suggested Prayer: Thank you, God, for the gift of loving people who have enriched our lives and our working years.

Remember the Benefits

Bible Reading: Psalm 103:1–6

These days it seems like everyone is worried about benefits. As I write, Congress is debating medical care reforms, and many are afraid of losing health care benefits. What is going to happen to Social Security, Medicare, Medicaid, unemployment insurance, medical insurance, and other benefits we have learned to depend on for security, especially in old age? When applying for a job, often the first concern is "What are the benefits offered with this employment?"

Earthly benefits may be awarded or revoked, according to the business guidelines or whims of the employer. The benefits that are ours in Christ, however, will never be withdrawn. They are always there for our taking—forgiveness, healing, redemption, compassion, satisfaction, renewal, peace, grace, hope, love, justification, reconciliation, and salvation. All are abundant and free.

In addition, Jesus promised, "Lo, I am with you always." Where else can you get benefits to match these?

—Eva Brightup

Song: "Jesus Never Fails"

A Suggested Prayer: Lord, your presence and promises are our security now and forever. We will not fear.

Looking Forward

Bible Reading: Ecclesiastes 11:1–6

"Cast your bread on the surface of the waters, for you will find it after many days." (Ecc. 11:1 [NASB])

I lost my life partner in death four years ago. We had enjoyed sixty-three years together, reveling in our family of four children, twelve grandchildren and eight great-grands (now eleven). Margaret enjoyed good health most of those years and was a marvelous cook and hostess. We entertained friends at our table again and again. But the last four or five years were hard on her, with two hip replacements and a triple bypass heart surgery. She came through it all with courage and victory. We felt God's sustaining hand in it all.

Now, I live alone. And life is lonely, despite TV, good books, friends, and long walks—especially after sixty-three years with so many golden moments. Then ... a ray of hope.

One of my sons is married to a Filipina woman. He suggested that I visit the Philippines, her homeland, to meet a possible family friend. I did, and soon, as God leads, I may have a companion once again.

Memories are precious. I'll never forget Margaret and our love for each other. But life flows on. She would be the first to say, "Go for it, Ray." I walk with God each day and seek his will. I wonder what God has for me.

—Raymond S. Nelson, Wichita, KS

Song: "Day by Day"

A Suggested Prayer: Lord, I commit my life to you, once again. Thank you for bringing me to this moment, living in a free land, enjoying a generous measure of health, wealth, and security. Lead me further into your glorious future.

The Calm at the Center

Bible Reading: Matthew 11:28–30

"Take the train from London to Dover and then board the Hovercraft to cross the English Channel." That sounded simple enough for spending a day in France with our tour group of college students and our three children.

If you are unfamiliar with the Hovercraft, it is a large boat-like conveyance that serves as a ferry, carrying vehicles and people across the twenty-some miles separating England and France. It doesn't actually rest in the water, as with a regular boat; it instead rides just above the surface on a huge cushion of air.

We were all anxious to get seats near windows on either end so we could enjoy the view, but our fun was short-lived. The sea was rough, and soon we began reaching for sickness bags strategically placed in the pockets on the backs of the seats ahead of us. It was with great relief that we felt the huge balloon beneath us deploy to land us gently on the shore of France.

Later that night, we dragged our weary bodies back on board a returning craft and fell into the nearest seats, well placed in the center. In *that* location we were gently rocked to sleep by the motion of the water.

How often I fret and worry, when Jesus said, "Come to me and I will give you rest." Ah, the calm at the center! When I keep Christ in the center of life I can rest in trust.

—Eva Brightup

Song: "It Is Well with My Soul"

A Suggested Prayer: In the midst of this day, be it calm or tumultuous, thank you for that peaceful center where you are in control.

Worry

Bible Reading: Luke 12:22–31

We have tried to feed birds during the winters for about three or four years. About all we are able to attract are sparrows. Jesus said sparrows don't worry about their future, for God feeds them, so we shouldn't worry. Probably no one works harder than the average sparrow to make a living! And this may be the point in Jesus's teaching: worry is not necessary if we work and do our best to handle the problems of life.

An experienced physician decided to analyze the "worriers" who were his patients. He found that 40 percent of them were apprehensive over things that never happened. About 30 percent concerned themselves with past matters now beyond their control. Another 12 percent anxiously feared the loss of their health, although their only illness was in their imagination. And the rest worried about their families, friends, and neighbors, but in most cases he discovered no basis for their fears.

Once, years ago, someone said, "What does your anxiety do? It does not empty tomorrow of its sorrow, but it does empty today of its strength. It does not make you escape the end; it makes you unfit to cope with it when it comes. God gives us the power to bear all the sorrow of his making, but he does not guarantee to give us strength to bear the burdens of our own making such as worry induces."

A humorous old saying comes to my mind: "Don't tell me that worry doesn't do any good. I know better. The things I worry about don't happen."

Worry is merely unbelief in God, parading in disguise.

—Harold B. Winn, *Friend to Friend*, p. 97
(Used with permission)

Song: "My Soul Has Found a Resting Place"

A Suggested Prayer: Lord, you have told us to cast all our cares upon you. May my soul rest in that place today.

Believing without Seeing

Bible Reading: Hebrews 11:1–10; Jeremiah 29:11

After living in parsonages for forty-six years, with eighteen years in the last one, my husband and I felt God leading us to do something different. The church year ended in June, so we gave our resignation letter the prior September. That would give the church—and us—plenty of time to make plans for the future. We didn't have a big retirement fund, so we needed income to buy our first home.

God gave us wonderful promises of his care, including Jeremiah 29:11. We felt very confident, but after eight months with no job or home, it got harder to believe without seeing. People offered many suggestions, including living in their basement. At last, in June, my husband was given a position at a manufacturing plant as chaplain, a wonderful place to pastor (his love)—and without board meetings.

We found a home, but it was too expensive and not finished. Since no pastor had been found, we were allowed to stay in the parsonage another month. Then we drove by a three-year-old house, identical to the one we'd found earlier, but it had a fenced yard and the cost was several thousand dollars less. We moved on July 31 and wondered how we could have had those moments of frustration and doubt.

We are grateful that God's promises are true, even if we have to wait until the last minute to see results with our physical eyes. They remained true as he helped us adjust to a new town, a new home, a new job, and a new church—a complete change in our lives.

The world says, "Seeing is believing," but we all know that it's not God's way. He tells us that he has plans to prosper us and give us a hope and a future (Jer. 29:11 [NIV]). Evangelist and author Beth Moore says we shouldn't confuse God's silence with inactivity. God wants us to believe without seeing.

—Elda Ann Cox, Wichita, KS.

Song: "He Leadeth Me"

A Suggested Prayer: Oh, Lord, help me to remember that the sun is always there, even when I can't see it. You are working, even when I see nothing happening.

Basket 9
Growing Spiritually

Kindergarten Theology

Bible Reading: Ephesians 3:14–19

John McCutcheon, contemporary folk music singer and writer, sings a tune about lessons he learned in kindergarten that have retained value for life up to the present. Some of the things he cites are how to tie his shoes, how to pose for a picture without a goofy grin on his face, and to remember to wash his hands before he eats.

Further, John mentions lessons regarding relationships, such as not hurting others, cleaning up after yourself, and holding hands with a friend when you are in dangerous or scary places.

Other advice he gives has to do with well-being, like looking before you cross the street and—my favorite—"Take a nap every day."

John also remembers a lesson that is probably common to all of us: planting a seed in a cup, waiting for roots to grow, and watching for the plant to pop through the soil. If we watered it too much or too little, the roots never formed, and the green never showed up.

The scripture above speaks of "being rooted and established in love."(NIV) We never get too old to need to tend the roots of our life in Christ. As with the plant in the cup, only when the root is healthy will the plant be strong.

—Eva Brightup

Song: "How Firm a Foundation"

A Suggested Prayer: May my life in secret with you spring forth in life that touches others with beauty and grace.

Obedience

Bible Reading: Psalm 32:8

When vacationing in 1984, I awakened with a full-blown idea of a way to minister to ministers: provide a place for them to get away to be with the Lord. The dream seemed important so I wrote down the details. It seemed like something my wife, Earlene, and I should do. We prayed about it, shared the idea with others, and eventually, there came a God-given name: "Shepherd's Rest."

When I retired from the Wichita Schools in 1991, the retreat still had not come to pass. It seemed like the idea might have to be developed by others. Then in 1997, we were able to buy property that could be used for this purpose. It is in a quiet, rural setting on an all-weather (unpaved) road near Wichita, Kansas. Our two-thirds–acre property, Shepherd's Rest, has a one-bedroom house (with a double bed) with central air and heating. It is free for pastors and anyone recommended by a pastor.

We are both in our late seventies; I have experienced two strokes (both a blockage and a hemorrhage), and my wife has recovered from a broken leg, but we are so happy that this retreat has been used by more than five hundred different people from various denominations and locations during the more than twelve years that it has been available. Although it's a fifty-mile round trip for the two of us, it is near our daughter and son-in-law. They keep the grass mowed and usually take care of "day-users." We take over when users stay overnight or longer.

We have learned from this experience to be patient. It may take several years for a God-given idea to be implemented.

—Benny Mevey, Wichita, KS

Editors' note: Benny died of cancer while this book was in progress.

Song: "Gentle Shepherd"

A Suggested Prayer: Help me to be obedient, even when there are delays.

Sauerkraut

Bible Reading: Psalm 143:8–10

Homemade sauerkraut is almost a thing of the past. I once saw [my friends] the Boehms making it. Ruth was cutting the cabbage heads in thirds, and Orren was pushing them through the kraut-cutter into a large tub. Whenever the tub got full, Orren would put a good bit of salt on the cabbage and work it in. Then he put the cabbage in a large five-gallon crock. When the crock was full and the preparation was finished, they laid leaves of cabbage on top and then put a large plate on this. They told me that if the weather was favorable, it would keep for several months just this way.

The kraut-cutter they used is an antique, and I expect for most Americans, making kraut is a thing of the past. All of us in this generation have gone a long ways from doing things the way our forefathers did them. I often wonder whether we are better men and women than our grandparents were. We have stopped doing a good many things they did all the time and we have started doing things that they would never have thought of doing. For example, there was a time when families had time to pray together before they went out to their responsibilities for the day. I read recently about a college student who was asked what he missed most about home, and after some hesitation he said, "The mornings when we as a family would join hands and pray before we had breakfast."

This is the kind of a thing that has been left behind, but it has robbed us of our inner strength to face life and its problems. "The family that prays together, stays together."

—Harold B. Winn, *Friend to Friend*, p. 85
(Used with permission)

Song: "Whisper a Prayer"

A Suggested Prayer: Lord, your blessings are new every morning. May our thankful hearts be lifted to you each day.

Jesus Goes to Yard Sales

Bible Reading: Matthew 5:14–16

As my husband and I grow older, our children keep reminding us that we need to get rid of excess things we have accumulated so they won't have to do it later. When we remember the days of labor it took to sort, give, and sell Grandpa and Grandma's collections, we agree with our children wholeheartedly. Don't ask, however, how we are progressing with the job.

Some time ago I came across an article by Mark Burrows in my Christian journal *Weavings*. It was titled "When Jesus Goes to Yard Sales." We would probably do well to have a few yard sales of our own, but what kind of yard sale would Jesus be interested in?

As I think of it, I'm sure I am hoarding some things Jesus would be happy to take off my hands. There is my need for human recognition and approval, my lack of trust that results in fear of the future, even my own righteousness that Isaiah 64:6 calls "filthy rags." My unloving attitudes and failure to forgive need to be placed on the table for disposal also. Then, there are those things Jesus has already paid for by his death and resurrection, and I simply need to give them up—things like my sin, guilt, and shame.

Maybe your spiritual closets, like mine, contain some things you don't need anymore. Why not bring them out into the light where Jesus can take them away in a "soul-cleaning" yard sale? You will be well paid with joy and freedom from excess baggage that is only a burden to carry.

—Eva Brightup

Song: "Whiter than Snow"

A Suggested Prayer: Lord, help me to give you those things in my life that get in the way of your radiance shining through me.

Christian Growth

Bible Reading: II Peter 3:18; Ecclesiastes 2:26

Nature divides each year into definite seasons. I especially enjoy the springtime. It is a time of renewal with warmer days, budding trees and plants, and welcome rains. The soil, especially if enriched with fertilizer and some gardening skills, can bring forth bounteous crops and beautiful flowers.

In most gardens, however, there are a few plants that do not seem to grow and flourish to look like the illustration on the seed package. While most of them seem to develop as they should, these plants just seem to "sit there," content to be as they are.

Perhaps some of us are somewhat like those garden plants. We have the opportunity to develop, to grow, to enlarge our understanding of what it means to live the Christian life, but we do not "bear much fruit" in our Christian experience. The Bible, good literature, the church, worship, and study are available, but we seem to lack the desire and vigor to use them and so we remain listless, disinterested, and inert.

The Christian life is the most challenging and rewarding experience in the world! At any age, it is our privilege and duty to grow in the grace and knowledge of God. The opportunity for growth is readily available to each of us. I pray that you will not be the "droopy plant" in God's garden!

—Faye McCoy, *One Generation*, p. 12
(Used with permission)

Song: "In the Garden"

A Suggested Prayer: Thank you for the opportunity to walk with you and talk with you on a daily basis. I pray my life will be enriched to bring forth much good fruit.

The Grace of Manure

Bible Reading: Luke 13:1–9

Luke 13 opens with a pronouncement of judgment that sounds harsh and final, but these words are followed immediately with a parable of grace available through repentance. The owner of the fig tree wanted to cut the fig tree down because it had borne no fruit. The compassionate gardener pled for one more chance to dig around it and fertilize it.

According to Sara Covin Juengst in her book *Like a Garden: A Biblical Spirituality of Growth*, this is the only biblical reference to using manure as a symbol for grace. Every gardener knows what manure can do for a garden.

Sometimes in life we may feel like we have had a whole load of manure dumped on us. It is easy to whine and complain ("Why me?"), instead of submitting to the gardener's digging and fertilization. Ironically, it seems that often the hard places in life lead to spiritual growth. Perhaps it is when we have come to the end of our own resources that we cling more closely to Jesus, who describes himself as "the vine."

Look for the grace in your load of manure, and you may be surprised at the growth and fruit that is produced.

—Eva Brightup

Song: "'Are Ye Able?' Said the Master"

A Suggested Prayer: Lord, help us to cling ever tighter to the vine, especially in our times of painful cultivation.

Summertime and the Livin' Is Easy ... Sometimes

Bible Reading: Luke 6:43–45

A few years ago—okay, a lot of years ago—when I was young, I looked forward to summer. No school. Time to read library books. Play hide-and-seek and catch lightning bugs after dark. Sleep in mornings while the air was cooler. Sleep in—that is, until my mother announced fruit picking and canning day. We must be in the orchard soon after daylight, before the heat of the day was upon us. Our instructions were: "Pick only the mature, ripe fruit and don't pad your bucket with diseased, over-ripe, rotting fruit."

Jesus's story about fruit says that good things come out of good stored in the heart, and likewise, bad fruit comes from bad. Hopefully, during our lives we have been storing good fruit, but if not, it is not too late to start. Whatever is grown inside is precisely what will come out. It isn't about simply looking good; it's about nurturing good from the inside out.

—Eva Brightup

Song: "Make Me a Blessing"

A Suggested Prayer: May we bring forth an abundance of good from the richness you have planted and nurtured within us.

Growing

Bible Reading: Ephesians 4:11–15

Are we ever really grown up? We say that we are by the time we have achieved our full physical growth, usually in the adolescent years, but is this what is meant by being grown up? Does "growing up" include growing spiritually as well as physically?

In Luke 1:80, we find that John "grew and developed in body and spirit," and in Luke 2:52, we are told that "Jesus grew both in body and in wisdom, gaining favor with God and men." (TEV) It would seem, according to the scripture, that growth is spiritual, as well as physical, and that it is continuous.

It's important to have a point in one's life to which one can refer and say, "This is where my life took on new meaning," or "This was the turning point in my life," but it is not enough to stop there, because life does go on, and one's spiritual pilgrimage never ends. As we look back, we can see our failures and our triumphs mirrored in the crooks and turns, the rough and the smooth places on the road. As we look ahead with our yet unfulfilled hopes, the way is not always clear, but the Light is there, and we move on with courage.

Along the way there have been people helping us. Perhaps they were unaware that they, by their very being, changed the course of our lives, and we were never the same afterward. Personal experiences of loss and failure have proven to be times of growth as we acknowledged the presence of God in our lives and let him work with us in bringing meaning and understanding to even our saddest and more devastating experiences.

Through it all, God has been and is guiding us, and for this we give heartfelt thanks. It is good to be alive and growing.

—Ruth Day, *Refreshings*, pp. 3–4
(Used with permission)

Song: "I Am Thine, O Lord"

A Suggested Prayer: In these later years of my life, Lord, help me continue to seek spiritual growth and development.

Basket 10
Improving Character

Put the Best Construction on Others' Actions

Bible Reading: Ephesians 1:15–19a

A comment made at the table this noon when one person remarked that young people today "just don't acknowledge gifts they receive," prompted some thinking tonight.

When one becomes old, it's easy to focus on one's slights by others, intentional or unintentional, and on the ingratitude of others, imagined or actual. When this happens, we become unlovely people; others anticipate time spent with us only with a sigh.

In regard to what we perceive to be the ingratitude of others, particularly when it concerns some service given, gift sent and not acknowledged, or help provided, would we not do well to remember and adopt Albert Schweitzer's philosophy? He said as he looked back over his life and recalled the number of people who had helped him in one way or another, he was astonished, humbled, and even shamed. Shamed because he realized how few knew how grateful he was; he had never expressed his gratitude, not because he wasn't grateful—he was; but he simply hadn't voiced his appreciation and sometimes out of shyness. Then he moved on to say he would venture many others probably were like him; and that being the case, we justifiably can face the world seeing it filled not with self-centered, ungrateful people but rather peopled with truly grateful and appreciative individuals.

If, in our older years, we embraced this philosophy, would we not engage in considerably less talk about people, and especially "this younger generation" being so ungrateful?

—Mildred Tengbom, *Moving*, pp. 193–194
(Used with permission)

Song: "Count Your Blessings"

A Suggested Prayer: Lord, give me a heart of gratitude for all your many blessings, including those that come to me through others of your children.

Pop Quiz

Bible Reading: Galatians 5:22–23

A few years ago, while returning in early April from a winter vacation in Florida, my wife and I were unexpectedly slowed by a glut of traffic traveling north on Highway I-75 from Naples to Tampa. We completed one twenty-five–mile stretch in seventy-five minutes. Slogging along with other travelers at a few miles per hour does not enhance my blood pressure, and at our age, blood pressure can be an issue.

Patience has never been one of my virtues. During my career years, I generally adhered to management consultant Peter Drucker's admonition: "Don't take any longer to make a decision than it takes to reverse it, should you later find out it was wrong."

This impatience has occasionally overflowed into my spiritual life. I have at times attacked prayer as if it were a duty to be accomplished, expecting the Lord to respond within the time that I had allotted for that task, and then naively wondered why our heavenly Father seemed to be "out to lunch."

I have often asked the Lord to teach me patience, and that request has been repeated far too often after I have failed to be adequately patient. Then one day, the Holy Spirit called to my attention that I had asked the

Lord to teach me patience, and that every day there seemed to be a pop quiz. He reminded me that the pop quiz was just that—a test, an opportunity to put into practice what I was being taught. This opened a whole new view of irritating circumstances, irritating people, and even temptation.

Under our heavenly Father's loving tutelage, this heretofore shriveled fruit of the Spirit (Galatians 5:22–23 [NIV]) has been growing—somewhat erratically at times but growing.

—Earl Brightup, St. Louis, MO

Song: "Teach Me, Lord, to Wait"

A Suggested Prayer: O Lord, teach me patience, and help me not to get impatient during the training.

Do You Have Hardening of the Oughteries?

Bible Reading: Psalm 63:1–8

Dudley Hall, in his book *Grace Works*, suggests that the reason some Christians look so miserable is that they are suffering from "hardening of the oughteries." They are always troubled about what they or others "ought" to have done or not have done. The truth is that we can never "do" enough to win favor with God. Hall suggests that we were not created for service but for fellowship with our heavenly Father. Appropriate service results from that relationship.

In the parable of the prodigal son (Luke 15:11–32), the older son seems to think he should be the favored son because he has *done* all the right things. He says, "Look, all these years I have worked for you like a slave." Duty had apparently replaced relationship. He continues, "I have never disobeyed your orders" (Luke 15:29 [TEV]). Simply keeping the rules easily leads to self-righteousness and missing the joy of fellowship. The son was so absorbed with *doing* all the right things that he completely missed the joy of *being* a son with access to all his father's resources.

There are no medical tests that I know of to diagnose "hardening of the oughteries." However, when religion (in some way doing all the right stuff) begins to overshadow relationship (doing the right things because they grow out of our intimate fellowship with God), then we may have serious symptoms of this insidious ailment. Perhaps it's time for a checkup.

—Eva Brightup

Song: "I Am Thine, O Lord"

A Suggested Prayer: I come into your presence today for the sheer joy of being with you and sitting at your feet.

Raspberries

Bible Reading: Galatians 6:7–9

A year ago this past spring, a friend gave us several red raspberry bushes. They started bearing in the middle of July and provided all the berries we wanted all summer and fall. Later, I bought a dozen black raspberry bushes and planted them beside the red raspberries. Later, Raymond told me that this wouldn't work. He said, "The red raspberries will do something to the black raspberries that kills them." I intended to move the black raspberry bushes but didn't get it done. Raymond asked me this spring if I had moved them, and I assured him that I was going to get it done. But I didn't! (They were doing fine where they were, and it could be that this wasn't always true.)

Both the red and the black started producing abundantly about the middle of June. When I returned from a trip at the end of June, those black raspberry bushes were either dead or dying.

This reminded me of life. There are many these days who think the older generation doesn't know anything. Time will prove that experience, which the older generation has, is right! There are many who think that the Bible is just an old-fashioned book with no relevance. They ignore it or secretly don't believe it, and then when they are just about ready to enjoy their pleasures and achievements, life dries up and dies like my berry bushes.

A man I tried to help told me that he could live the way he wanted to, regardless of what the Bible said. He got drunk one night and committed a crime. The judge sentenced him from one to ten years in prison. He didn't have to listen to the Bible, but he couldn't escape the blight of sin's wages.

I didn't have to move the berry bushes, but I am not getting any black raspberries either!

—Harold B. Winn, *Friend to Friend*, p. 69
(Used with permission)

Song: "Savior, Lead Me Lest I Stray"

A Suggested Prayer: I am safe in the hollow of your hand. Keep me there, lest I wander into dangerous territory.

The Hard Steel of Personality—1

Bible Reading: Proverbs 4:23

His name was Bill. As the pastor of a congregation, a member had asked me to stop in a nursing home and visit with Bill. I went with questions in my mind! Upon our meeting, the conversation went something like this:

"Hello, Bill. My name is Lowell Weinacht. A friend of mine asked me to visit with you. Is that okay?"

"Sure is. I am always glad to talk with believers!" Bill had been a man of the world and had lived the life of the world. He had been a lumberjack (he still had the stature) and had lived the reputed lifestyle.

But through his tears, he shared with me, "One day I saw my life of sin with horror and repentance!" The rest of our conversation was filled with joy, laughter, thanksgiving, praise, and prayer.

A hard personality, even in older years, when honest before God, can still say yes and no with passion. I still remember Bill as a "brother of passion." Let us all be passionate about our love for Christ!

—Lowell Weinacht, Nampa, ID

Editors' Note: Lowell died unexpectedly a few days after submitting his material.

Song: "Give Thanks"

A Suggested Prayer: Lord, I give thanks for Bill and for all who call upon your name in truth and in love.

The Hard Steel of Personality—2

Bible Reading: Proverbs 4:23

His name I do not remember; his clear, deep blue eyes I do. As a pastor, I was visiting in a nursing home, and the staff asked me to visit with a man whom I named "Mr. Blue Eyes." He was just being admitted.

As I walked into his room, he lay with his back to me, facing a wall. I introduced myself. He did not answer, but I knew he heard me. After speaking to him for a while, I asked the question that emitted a response: "Do you have any interest in your spiritual life, of knowing God?"

He stirred and, with effort, turned to face me. I saw those clear blue eyes. He answered with a firm and strong voice, "Not at all!" One week later, he died of cancer.

I am not being judgmental, for I did not know the man. This is not to say he was a bad person; he simply had a strong personality and made firm decisions.

I am reminded that in our older years, we depict and display our character with a new and often stronger vigor, whether we are believers or non-believers. How about your heart? Is it strong for God?

—Lowell Weinacht, Nampa, ID

Song: "How about Your Heart?"

A Suggested Prayer: Lord, make me sensitive to the leading of your spirit in heart and actions.

How's Your Eyesight?

Bible Reading: Psalm 71:14–18

Opening the daily *Wichita Eagle,* a large headline caught my eye: **"Presbyopia—'old eyes'—is inevitable. Here's how to deal with it."** Unfortunately, the rest of the article was in regular newsprint size, perfectly illustrating for some of us the message of the headline.

Sight is perhaps the one of the five senses that we tend to value the most. My own father underwent four elective eye surgeries after his ninetieth birthday in order to improve and preserve his ability to see.

In John 9, the story is recorded of Jesus's healing a man who had been blind from birth. The disciples asked, "Who sinned, this man or his parents that he should be born blind?" Jesus answered, "It was neither…,but it was in order that the works of God might be displayed in him." (John 9:2-3 [NASB])

As we grow older and various body parts begin to fail, we sometimes have trouble acknowledging that the work of God can still be displayed in us. However, he has been working on us our whole lives to make us into the persons we are today and, if we are still living and pliable, he isn't done with us yet. God's goal is to make us more and more like himself.

Failing body parts may become less important as we submit to God's handiwork in our spirits. There is still important work to be done—perhaps with less activity but important, nonetheless—to loved ones, friends, those in Christian ministries, and all whom we support in prayer and encouragement. May we be faithful to continue demonstrating the work of God every moment we are granted on this earth.

—Eva Brightup

Song: "Be Thou My Vision"

A Suggested Prayer: Reveal to us your ways, Lord, and make us faithful distribution points for your love in the world.

Basket 11
Feeling Discontent

Mosquitoes That Buzz and Annoy

Bible Reading: I Peter 5:6–10

Luverne, [my husband], is back in the classroom, teaching part-time, attending meetings, and filling up his appointment book. Life as usual for him, I think, but not for me. After one or one's loved one has had an encounter with a life-threatening disease, accident, or illness, some things change. For me, life has assumed a tentativeness it did not have before. I am restless. Decisions I have resisted making in the past command attention from me; questions that formerly I had pushed to the back of my mind now insist on claiming my attention.

Luverne soon will be seventy. When will he retire from his teaching position at the institute? We both have been blessed in being able to work at vocations we love; and retiring from a job one has loved can be difficult, I know. The temptation may come to wonder what meaning life can hold afterwards, but doesn't the time come when we need to walk away from the podium, the computer, the desk, the farm, the office, the pulpit, wherever we've pursued our career, and instead discover new interests?

We need to decide where we want to spend our later years. How long do we want to continue living in this 3000-square-foot house? Clean it? Repair it? Live in this neighborhood? Do we want to wait to move until our physical strength will be diminished, until we will find it difficult to make friends in a new setting?

The trouble is, Luverne doesn't want to discuss it. Whenever I bring up the subject, he swats it away as though it's an annoying mosquito. How can we reach a decision that will please or at least be acceptable to both of us? Troubled, I turn to a prayer in our Book of Worship: "O most loving Father and God, you want me to give thanks for all things, to fear nothing except losing you, and to lay all my cares on you, knowing you care for me. Help me to do just that, O my God."

—Mildred Tengbom, *Moving*, pp. 39–42
(Used with permission)

Song: "Anywhere with Jesus"

A Suggested Prayer: Most loving Father and God, help me to lay all my cares on you, knowing you care for me.

Are You Discouraged?

Bible Reading: Philippians 4:6–7; John 14:27

Don't be misled by the constant din of discouraging news that is part of daily life. It is there in the media, in conversation, and in attitude. I recall an incident that took place in Spivey, Kansas, the community where I grew up.

This was many years ago in the Spivey State Bank. The cashier was a very personable, popular, and jolly young man who loved practical jokes. One day the tables were turned by the local citizens, who were instructed to make a point of going to the bank and mentioning how "bad" the cashier looked. They managed to convince him that he was really ill. By mid-afternoon he dragged himself home and collapsed on the divan. His "suffering" came to an unexpected climax when his friends rushed in, hilarious at the success of their trick!

It is easy for us to fall into the same trap! It is true that there are disturbing situations all around us, but as Christian people we have an inner peace that is with us at all times. Jesus is always near. He is there for our strength in any circumstance, so do not despair when things seem to be in turmoil.

Remember that there are situations that are unpleasant or worrisome, but with the assurance that Jesus is near us wherever we are, each of us can cope. What other persons do or say or think need not influence us. We are able, with God's help, to deal with individual problems. Depend on God's wisdom. Keep your attitude in line with God's teaching. Rest in assurance from the words from the Bible.

—Faye McCoy, *One Generation*, p. 28
(Used with permission)

Song: "Wonderful Peace"

A Suggested Prayer: Prince of Peace, calm my fearful and fretting heart.

Songs in the Night

Bible Reading: Ecclesiastes 12:1–4

In Ecclesiastes 12:4, a metaphorical picture of old age, the writer says the elderly one awakens at the sound of a bird. This could depict either an early riser or a light sleeper (both common to old age). As I've grown older I have discovered I don't rest as well as I did in younger years, when I used to fall into bed, fatigued from late-night work, and be asleep instantly.

Now, I often waken in the night and cannot go back to sleep. Sometimes I'm disturbed by a troubling TV story or news item I saw before going to bed. Sometimes my mind struggles with an unresolved issue or problem in my life. Sometimes it is simply a senseless worry. These times of wakefulness are not welcome, and I try to avoid them.

Sometimes, however, there is a persistency, as if God is trying to get my attention. In these instances, the stillness of the night has provided a wonderful opportunity for spiritual refreshing, as I have prayed for some family member or bathed some upcoming issue in prayer. Sometimes I have been provided a solution or a new approach or clarity regarding a confusing situation.

In these restless hours, I often discover that the words of some hymn keep circling through my mind, a hymn of confidence or praise. Job 35:10 refers to "God, who gives songs in the night" (some Bible versions translate the word as "strength" rather than "songs"). I have often felt that the circling song was a divine gift, providing comfort and allowing me to fall back to sleep to enjoy rest for the balance of the night.

—Leroy Brightup

Song: "Redeemed" (note the last verse)

A Suggested Prayer: O, God, in our restless nights (and days), visit us with your joy and peace.

The Battle with a Sense of Worthlessness

Bible Reading: Romans 8:38–39

Joseph, [a neighbor], was "down" today. He complained that he wasn't good for anything anymore, that he couldn't do anything, and that he never would be able to do anything again.

I listened, then moved over to the patio door and stood looking outside. After a while he asked me what I was thinking about. I told him he doesn't like being preached at. He was silent and then said, "Well, I could try it." I said no. I heard a chuckle, then, "Oh, come on. Just once."

I waited, then turning, walking up to his bed and looking him in his eye, kindly, I hoped, I said, "Joseph, what we *are* is far more important than anything we *do*."

Silence. A steady gaze returned. Then, "Thank you, Millie."

No more gloomies, at least for today. But I certainly can understand his feelings. Who of us hasn't felt the same?

—Mildred Tengbom, *Moving*, p. 138
(Used with permission)

Song: "I'm a Child of the King"

Prayer Suggestion: Pray for the right words to speak today to bring encouragement to someone for whom life seems bleak.

Feeling Lonely

Bible Reading: Hebrews 13:5b–6

I was feeling lonely again today but reminded myself I've known times in the past when vagrant, troublesome feelings of loneliness have haunted me, even when I've been at a party or have gathered for a family reunion. Sometimes in fact, those occasions can be the loneliest.

However, I also know from experience I can do something about these feelings, and so today I picked up the phone and made three dates to meet friends for lunch or an evening meal. Before we moved here some of our friends had asked if they could come for a housewarming when we were settled. I called one of them today, too, and said, "Come! Please do!" So now we have four happy events to which we can look forward.

—Mildred Tengbom, *Moving*, p. 127
(Used with permission)

Song: "I'm So Glad I'm a Part of the Family of God"

A Suggested Prayer: Lord, give me eyes to envision ways I might bring relief from loneliness to friends of mine, and in so doing, find joy myself also.

Everything Belongs

Bible Reading: Romans 8:28–39

About three years ago, when I first entered an especially troubling time in my life, I hardly knew what to do. I was under stress, out of balance, upset, obsessed, and mildly depressed. I did not lose faith or hope but rather continued my spiritual disciplines of Bible reading, journaling, and prayer.

During this time an encouraging and helpful thought came from the writings of Richard Rohr in his book *Everything Belongs*. His main point is that everything which comes into the life of a committed Christian is used for God's glory and our spiritual growth. If everything belongs in our life, then God is in the hard times as well as the good. He is with us to help us. Our job is to seek his face and his will in what is happening. We have the promise of [the above] Bible reading: "And we know that God causes everything to work together for the good of those who love God and are called according to his purpose for them" (NLT).

God is with us in every unsettling circumstance or bewildering happening. He is also in every joyful occasion or fulfilling incident. He has called us for a high and holy purpose. As we keep our focus on him, no one or no thing can defeat us or deter us in our Christian walk. We are enabled to keep the right perspective.

Everything does belong!

—Robert A. Crandall, *Fruit*, vol. 49, no. 4, p. 30
(Used with permission)

Song: "The Love of God"

A Suggested Prayer: Lord, though I can't understand all that is happening, I know that because of your love, it will work for my good.

Feeling at Home

Bible Reading: Genesis 12:1–4

"Do you feel at home now when you come back to Pilgrim Place [a retirement center] after having been away?" one of our friends asked.

"It's better now," I answered, but when I am alone I ask myself if I can ever expect to feel at home here or anyplace else. The Children of Israel lived for years in Babylon. ... I think those of us who have moved often and lived in many different places ... have felt as though we were continually moving from one Babylon to another. That being the case, why should I not accept vagrant feelings of loneliness that pass through me as normal?

But no matter where we have lived I have tried to make a home for our family. ... But calling a place home does not mean all loneliness disappears. And in these, my latter years, should I be troubled if from time to time I do not feel at home? After all, "this world is not my home; I'm just a-passin' through."

Pilgrim Place probably will be the end of the journey for this aging, decaying body, but that will mark but the beginning of the journey God intended for us to make when he created us. When the last breath ceases or gasps its way out of this body, it only will mean ...

an exchange of planes. I don't really want to change planes yet; the flight I'm on pleases me.

But I am praying God will enable me to look forward more and more to my homegoing, when I shall know him more fully.

—Mildred Tengbom, *Moving*, pp. 200–201
(Used with permission)

Song: "This World Is Not My Home"

Prayer Suggestion: Pray today for someone whose present living arrangements are very disagreeable, making life unpleasant for him or her.

Basket 12
Seeing God's Work

The Wind Blows in Kansas and Elsewhere

Bible Reading: John 3:5–8

Our clock radio snapped on at 6:00 a.m. with the weather forecast: "Brisk, gusty winds from the south." So, what else is new in Kansas? I filed that bit of information in my brain and proceeded to get ready to go to work.

All morning the winds blew against the south window of my office. At lunchtime I left the building by way of the south door. Immediately, I was surprised to feel a strong wind against my back. Wind in the north? The forecaster had said strong *south* winds. How could this be? As I walked forward, I emerged from between two buildings and, suddenly, the wind hit me in the face. Apparently, the proximity of the two buildings shifted the wind current to make me sense it on my back.

I remembered reading of Jesus's description of the ways of the Spirit: "The wind blows wherever it pleases. You hear its sound, but you cannot tell where it comes from or where it is going. So it is with everyone born of the Spirit." (John 3:8 [NIV]) It seems that just when we think we have it all figured out, where and how God will act, we might be astonished to see him at work in a totally unexpected place or way.

So, we shouldn't be "blown away" to see the Holy Spirit at work in ways we have deemed unlikely or impossible.

—Eva Brightup

Song: "Surprise, Surprise, God Is a Surprise"

A Suggested Prayer: May I see the surprises you bring my way today and rejoice to see you at work.

An Answer to Prayer

Bible Reading: James 5:16

"The effectual fervent prayer of a righteous man availeth much" (James 5:16).

My doctors had told me kindly but firmly that there was no hope of my husband's recovery. He was living in the intensive care unit of a large hospital. He had a severe heart attack and three cardiac arrests and had been on complete life support machines for several days.

When he had his first attack and cardiac arrest, the doctors had worked hard for what seemed to be a long time to get him to breathe again, so they told me that if he should live a short while, he would have no mind, but the Lord gave me faith to believe he would, and I told the doctors so. They just patted my shoulder and promised to do all they could to help him.

He and I have many good Christian friends who visited him, and they all helped me pray and hold Homer up in love and prayers to the Lord. In about two or three weeks, he was up walking in the hall of the hospital, and he knew me and most everyone. Praise the Lord. A few days later I brought him home.

That was eight years ago, and today he is leading a fairly normal life. He and I go to church every Sunday.

He drives the car and does about anything he wants to, but he can't do hard work.

In six more months we will celebrate our fifty-seventh wedding anniversary. We pray each day and thank the Lord for his many blessings. We try to follow the model prayer and say, "Thy will be done."

—Mabel H. Wagoner, *Refreshings*, pp. 197–198
(Used with permission)

Song: "What a Friend We Have in Jesus"

Prayer Suggestion: Pray for someone experiencing a crisis in health or for a family who has lost a loved one by death recently.

Overcoming Joy

Bible Reading: Philippians 4:4–9

Several years ago my wife and I attended a retreat sponsored by a Christian institution. The speaker at the Sunday morning worship service was its president, who used [the above] Bible reading for his remarks. At that time he was facing an incurable malignancy. What would he say? With an overcoming certainty and energetic enthusiasm, he spoke of the challenge and courage for living each day with joy. He seemed to be content in the love and grace of God. Whenever I use this Bible reading, I remember his clear testimony.

There must have been some similar reason for the apostle Paul to place such an emphasis upon joy. Twice he urges the Philippians to "Rejoice in the Lord always." Perhaps it is in response to something the church was facing: difficult circumstances, disunity in the body, false teaching, or even persecution. Whatever the situation, they were encouraged to face it in the power of the risen and overcoming Lord Jesus.

The same resources are available and abundant for us today. First, there is prayer and petition, with thanksgiving. Then there is the peace of God that passes all understanding. Rather than anxiety and worry, we are to think on right and noble things. Finally, we are to put into practice what we know. Here, [Christian theologian and author] Richard Foster has a helpful reminder: "God's normal means of bringing us his joy is by redeeming and sanctifying the ordinary junctures of life" (*Celebration of Discipline*, p. 165).

May the joy of the Lord be your strength today!

—Robert A. Crandall, *Fruit*, vol. 49, no. 4, p. 32
(Used with permission)

Song: "Rejoice in the Lord Always"

A Suggested Prayer: Thank you for the peace and joy your presence brings, dear Lord. I rejoice in all your good gifts today.

God's Wonderful Mystery

Bible Reading: Colossians 1:24–27

Ever since I was a child, reading Nancy Drew and Hardy Boys books, I have loved a good mystery. A really good mystery book draws you into the plot on the very first page, and it doesn't release you until the solution is revealed in the final paragraphs.

It has occurred to me that the Bible, the record of God's dealings with humankind, is a mystery itself. The story begins on the first page: "In the beginning God created the heaven and the earth." I'm not so concerned with exactly *how* he did it. My question is *why* he did it.

All through the Old Testament record we are shown ways God chose to communicate with his people. Walking and talking with the great God of the universe is a huge and wonderful mystery to me, and yet he continually finds ways to let me know he is with me always.

The New Testament opens with the mystery of the Son of God coming to live among us, continues with the provision for our reconciliation to God through the death of his Son and the revelation of Colossians 1:27 that God has chosen to make known to the Gentiles the glorious riches of the mystery, "which is Christ in you, the hope of glory." John Calvin is quoted as having said he would rather experience than understand it. That we can do. We can experience the life of Christ living in us, the hope of glory!

—Eva Brightup

Song: "I Stand Amazed"

A Suggested Prayer: Thank you for daily experience with the living Christ.

Imagine That!

Bible Reading: Ephesians 1:18–19

Children seem to have no difficulty whatsoever using their imaginations. One evening we were caring for grandchildren, and Courtney was pretending I was her little girl, and I had been bad so she sent me to bed in her room. In her imagination, that was not sufficient punishment for my crime, so she further switched off the light and marched out of the room, closing the door. Terrible punishment for a tired old grandma!

Jesus told a number of stories that require us to use our imagination in order to get the point. Imagine picking a splinter out of another's eye while ignoring a log in your own, chopping off an arm, or poking out an eye if it causes you to sin.

The Ephesians scripture (NIV) speaks of what we might call "sanctified imagination"—the eyes of our hearts enlightened to know the hope we have in him, our glorious inheritance, and his great power available to us.

—Eva Brightup

Song: "Open My Eyes That I May See"

A Suggested Prayer: Enlighten our minds, God, to live every day in hope and in the rich inheritance and power we have in you.

Attentiveness

Bible Reading: Romans 8:12–17

The Lord has a way of getting our attention when we have a spiritual need. He showed me the solution to a weakness in my thinking and spiritual practices through a book I picked up in a home where we were visiting. Written by a medical doctor, one section dealt with how to reduce stress in one's life. He wrote that one helpful habit was "mindfulness," which he defined as "the practice of learning to pay attention to what is happening to you moment by moment."

Early in life I was taught that just as the physical life is one breath at a time, the Christian way is a moment-by-moment journey. But I haven't always followed that practice well. You see, I tend to think more about the past, evaluating what could have been done differently or to plan for the future for the best possible results. The problem is that I miss much of what God has for me right now.

As I wrestled with the excitement of new spiritual and emotional possibilities, the Holy Spirit reminded me of something Richard Foster had written regarding God's wanting us to be alert to all that is going on around us and to "discern the footprints of the holy" (*Prayer*, p. 28).

I hope you can join me in a new awareness of God at work. To live in the present is to live in God, for he is the eternal now.

—Robert A. Crandall, *Fruit*, vol. 49, no. 4, p. 28
(Used with permission)

Song: "Moment by Moment"

A Suggested Prayer: Lord, help me to be so in touch with the Spirit that I can receive all God has for me in this moment of life.

Basket 13
Keeping Healthy

Discipline

Bible Reading: I Corinthians 3:16

Oh, Lord, why am I depressed today? Why don't my children and grandchildren call me? Oh, Lord, why do I fight this weight battle? A negative response to these questions can steal my joy. Here are my five W's that help me with life struggles.

Worship: Sing or read the words of a worship song in a hymnal. Examples are "When Morning Guilds the Sky" and "Crown Him with Many Crowns." Worship him in the beauty of the sunrise or nature.

Word: My goal is to read some of his Word every day. The Psalms always speak to me in a new and fresh way. I have found focusing on memorizing his Word has been a strength in my life. Many times the Holy Spirit will bring just the right word to me to encourage me.

Walk: In my senior years I have found that I have to keep those body parts moving. I don't always feel like exercising, but if I discipline myself to do it, I feel much better overall and have more energy.

Water: Up to 60 percent of the human body is water. According to U.S. government statistics, the brain is composed of 70 percent water, the lungs are 90 percent water, and about 83 percent of our blood is water. So, I need to drink, drink, drink. Sometimes, if I am feeling tired, I will just drink several glasses of water, and I will feel better.

Way of Eating: Lord, help me to accept this season of my life. Teach me what my body needs to function at its best.

—Velda Kuhns, Wichita, KS

Song: "All the Way My Savior Leads Me"

Prayer Suggestion: Pray about areas of your life in which you may need to be more disciplined.

Health Care

Bible Reading: Mark 6:45, 53–56

For many months the United States has experienced turmoil regarding health care reform. All of us in the United States and other developed countries have come to expect good medical services as a right, rather than a privilege.

Advanced medical techniques have made possible treatment for physical ills that were undiagnosed or untreatable only a few years ago. Some ill persons live with the hope that a cure will yet be found before their illness claims their life.

Recently, following the removal of a decayed tooth, my jaw did not seem to heal. The dentist determined that the bone had separated, and I had a broken jaw. Through surgery, my jaw was set and stabilized with a metal rod and several screws, and healing began. All of this was accomplished through several visits to a highly trained oral surgeon, advanced x-ray technology, a surgically sterile operating room, and effective medication (and a lot of Jell-O and pudding).

During the many weeks of care, I became thankful for relief from pain, for correction of my problem, and the possibility of normal life again. My mind kept going to the same unsettling scenario: "What if I had lived in one of several countries where such healing arts and treatment are unavailable? What kind of a life could I have looked forward to?"

—Leroy Brightup

Song: "The Great Physician"

Prayer Suggestion: Pray for medical workers in mission hospitals and other locations where they daily serve masses of the ill with limited supplies and equipment.

Pain

Bible Reading: Revelation 21:1–7

It is not easy to define pain, but everyone knows what it is. There are so many kinds of physical pain: there is the pain of a burn, the pain of an incision, the pain of a chronic affliction, the pain that comes to a mother at birth, and the pain of a heart attack, cancer, and rheumatism, besides the many more humble and unromantic forms of pain.

Pain is not a pleasant subject, but there is good that comes out of it. Pain is a warning of danger or a symptom of something wrong in the body. When pain hits us, it is a signal made by the nerves, trying to get a message through to us that something needs attention.

The aftermath of pain should make us doubly thankful for health, strength, and physical well-being. Pain often puts us on our back and removes us from the whirlpool of activities. It provides opportunities for us to look up to God and care for some unfinished business with the Lord.

Once when I spoke about how unfortunate it was that a certain man had terminal cancer, one of the best surgeons in our district said to me, "This is not so bad. This gives a man time to care for any unfinished business with God."

I have thought about that several times! Pain does open the door for suffering people to draw nigh to God. It gives us a realization that life is uncertain, and we need to be certain about our spiritual condition preparatory for the next life.

One of the glories of heaven is the absence of pain. In the Bible we read: "And God shall wipe away all tears from their eyes; and there shall be no more death, neither sorrow, nor crying, neither shall there be any more pain" (Revelation 21:4).

—Harold B. Winn, *Friend to Friend*, pp. 49–50
(Used with permission)

Song: "When We See Christ"

A Suggested Prayer: Lord, we look forward to the day when we will be free from pain, but in the meantime, help us to be patient in allowing pain to do its work.

FAST

Bible Reading: Isaiah 53:1–5

Progress on writing and editing this book of devotionals was delayed due to an ischemic stroke (blockage or TIA) and recovery time. I had risen about 6:00 a.m. and gone to the basement bathroom to prepare for the day. An hour later, my wife found me unconscious on the bathroom floor. I had no warning sign of any problem. I only remember losing my balance and falling.

I did not recognize the signs of a stroke, but my wife did. I didn't think I needed help and begged her not to call 911, but she did, and the EMT crew was at our door almost immediately. I have since learned that there is a medication to help stroke victims, but for effectiveness, it has to be administered within three hours of having the stroke.

I was released from the hospital three days later with no long-term physical impairments, all thanks to God. I have my wife to thank for fast action. At the hospital I was taught the acronym FAST for recognizing a stroke. Although this is neither a medical book nor an advice column, I have become an evangelist for FAST, as fewer people recognize the signs of a stroke than those of a heart attack. The symptoms for which one should check, following the acronym, are:

F (face): Is there any unusual appearance of face or mouth (e.g., sagging lips or cheeks)?

A (arm): Is there any numbness, weakness, or inability to lift or move an arm?

S (speech): Is the person slurring words or exhibiting an inability to speak?

T (time): If any of the above symptoms are present, it's time to call 911.

As we age, we are more prone to some of these ailments, but fast action can spare us unnecessary misery.

—Leroy Brightup

Song: "The Healer"

Prayer Suggestion: Pray for someone you know whose quality of life has been reduced due to a sudden illness, such as a heart attack or stroke.

A Full-Length Mirror

Bible Reading: Genesis 1:26-31b; Psalm 113:1-3

If only we could see ourselves as others see us!

Spending our first winter as "snow birds" in Texas, the spacious ranch home—our home away from home for two months—had, as one feature, a full-length mirror positioned at the end of a long hallway. One's own image could not be avoided, as the hall led to the bedroom and bath assigned to us.

A bit of reality could not be avoided. Did I really walk like that? Did my shoulders really slump so? What about the casual wardrobe and coiffure that also was mirrored without any forgiving brush-lighted effect?

I instantly made attempts to get in shape; needed corrections more consistently were resolved. Alas, it was too easy to fall back into the comfort-zone patterns that were already in place. "I'll get a full-length mirror of my own as soon as we return home," I remember firmly declaring.

Today, there is no full-length mirror on a wall in our home. There is, however, an awareness of the value of caring for the earthly temple. Bodily discipline is of profit and is a reasonable requirement.

—Eloise Brown, Wichita, KS

Song: "Bless Thou the Lord, O My Soul"

Prayer Suggestion: Meditate on the words of the song "Jesus Will Walk with Me."

More Mirrors

Bible Reading: Matt. 6:26–30; 11:29–30

Remember when the family tape recorder was the communication device of choice for sending messages to loved ones who were unable to be present at a holiday gathering? I do. Hearing this valuable "gift" played back, unmistakably identifying one's own voice, was a reality check. "I don't sound like that, do I? Horrors!" I resolved to improve my high timbre, changing it to a more acceptable, mature tone.

When I feel the need for a lift in image, I like to peruse current style magazines and trends in fashions and personal care. In search of ideas, recently I purchased a popular issue in which there was a how-to section of personal care for women in their twenties, thirties, forties, and fifties, complete with illustrations. I found this section very intimidating. The sixties and up—where were they? Omitted. Apparently, the editor considered that women in their sixties and beyond were already accustomed to familiar comfort-wear and somewhat lacking in creativity. (My kind of person?) Once again, I had to rely on my own judgment for self-improvement!

Persistence paid off. On a shopping trip, I selected a few items, which I tried on in the dressing room—

complete with a three-way full-length mirror. The lighting revealed a variety of facial aging, lines, and flaws. Now I needed to find a cosmetic product for that—and a lighted magnifying bathroom mirror.

After further reflection, I am consoled by an inner persuasion that externals have value, but more to be sought is godliness with contentment, self-acceptance, individuality, maturity, and dignity.

—Eloise Brown, Wichita, KS

Song: "Dear Lord and Father of Mankind"

A Suggested Prayer: Help me consistently to radiate the love and spirit of Christ in my attitude and in all I do.

Basket 14
Finishing Well

Heaven

Bible Reading: John 11:20–27

A few weeks ago, [Bessie], our church treasurer, died. Her death was not expected; thus, it came as a shock. As her pastor, I stopped in to see her one evening just a few hours before she died. After I prayed for her and with her, she said something [that] I will always remember: "I see the mansions and they are so beautiful. I see Jesus." Soon after this, she went into a coma and, within a few hours, died. Bessie had served her Lord faithfully for many years. Thus, she died as she lived! She walked with her Lord in life, and in death, she had him to walk with her through the river of death.

Science is now telling us that the dying person is often the first to know that he is dying, and he recognizes and resents efforts to conceal the fact from him. This confirms my experience of being with many people in their last days and hours on earth.

To some, death [seems] mysterious and terrifying. Some accuse both physicians and clergymen of feeling uncomfortable with death. ... I must confess that it is much easier to be with godly people, like Bessie, when they die than it is to be with those who die cursing God and everyone around them.

The New Testament never uses "death" when referring to the end of a Christian's life on earth. It uses the word "sleep," giving the thought that there will be a resurrection morning when the Christian's body will be raised up, like we get up in the morning after a night's sleep. To go to bed at night is not terrifying. Thus, for the Christian who knows his Lord well enough to recognize him in the shadows, death is not a dreaded experience; it is moving from earth to heaven. The apostle Paul said, "To be absent from the body is to be present with the Lord" (II Cor. 5:8).

—Harold B. Winn, *Friend to Friend*, p. 71
(Used with permission)

Song: "I Know That My Redeemer Liveth"

A Suggested Prayer: Lord, because you live, we will live also. Give us confidence and assurance in our times of doubt and anxiety.

Useless Fears

Bible Reading: Psalm 46:1–7

Sometimes, like today, my friends in the hospital with whom I have visited do not speak of God helping them. He is, I am sure, but they have no awareness of it. Today only one troubled soul opened up and spoke about his distress, his fear of death.

I wonder how it will be for me when my time comes. Will I be consciously aware of God's help? He has promised he will never, never leave me nor forsake me, but … I remember the godly man who cried out in agony as he lay dying, because he said God had disappeared, gone into hiding; he couldn't feel his presence. That's hard both for the dying person and the family and friends standing by.

But I must not allow myself to focus on this! Instead, I must say to myself over and over, "Whether I am conscious or not of his presence, God *will* be with me. I can depend on him. All will be well."

[It helps also to know] that the suffering ones in my hospital and all the other hospitals and even care centers represent only a minority of the aged who suffer like these do. Many, many aged ones do die suddenly, in their sleep or peacefully at home.

I must let the unknown be just that—the unknown. I act foolishly if I add [fear] to my uneasiness about the unknown. And since I do not know what may lie ahead, why shouldn't I begin to live, seeing possibilities in the aging years, seeing them as liberating, not restricting; beneficial, not harmful; capable of producing personal growth, not limiting or destroying it?

—Mildred Tengbom, *Moving*, p. 111
(Used with permission)

Song: "I Know Who Holds Tomorrow"

A Suggested Prayer: Hear our prayer, Lord, and speak your peace to our fearful hearts.

Our Tombstone

Bible Reading: Psalm 89:1–2

In an effort to save our children some worry and expense at our death, my wife and I have purchased and set our gravestone beside the headstone of our first child, who died at birth. In trying to decide what we wanted etched on the stone, besides our names, we settled on including the date of our wedding and the names of our four children.

In addition, in the center we placed the word "Kept." The motto is short, but it is our witness to God's faithfulness through over fifty-five years of marriage. We've known some very deep sorrows, like losing our first baby. We've been on the edge financially. We've had all the typical trials in raising our family. But God has always been faithful to walk beside us in our grief or confusion. As we reflect on life together, we've been well cared for. We've been "kept."

"Kept" is also our witness to our faith regarding the future. Whatever death holds, we are confident our eternal life is in God's hands. Those who see our gravestone in the future will know our everlasting lives are held securely in his loving embrace—"kept."

—Leroy Brightup

Song: "Great Is Thy Faithfulness"

A Suggested Prayer: Your faithfulness to us throughout our lives leaves us standing in gratitude and awe. Thank you.

Finish the Job

Bible Reading: Acts 20:22–24

As a child, I lived with my family on a small farm in southeast Kansas. We didn't have many of the conveniences we think necessary today, things like running water, electricity, or indoor plumbing.

Our water had to be carried from the pump that stood on a cement pedestal in the northeast corner of our backyard, and it was often my job to pump and bring in the fresh supply. Many times I looked at the back door several yards away and wondered, "Will I ever get there with this heavy load?"

Our family was also blessed with an aunt who had Down syndrome. Aunt Blanche lived in a grown-up body but with a mind that was pretty much on a level with us kids. Sometimes she wanted to help bring in the water. She loved to pump the old handle up and down until her bucket was running over; then she would pick up the pail and start toward the house. After a few steps she would stop and pour out a little. A few more steps and it was still too heavy, so she tipped it up and let out a little more. By the time she got to the house, we were lucky to have a third to half of a bucketful.

As Paul said, his goal was to finish the race and complete the task given him by the Lord Jesus. No, we are not there yet. Completing the task may require some inconvenience, some discomfort of carrying a bucket that at times feels too heavy, but it will be worth it all if we finish the job successfully with the bucket still full!

—Eva Brightup

Song: "It Will Be Worth It All"

A Suggested Prayer: Lord, keep our eyes steady and our steps firm as we press toward the prize that is ours in Christ Jesus.

Near-Death Experiences

Bible Reading: Luke 8:1–3

In numerous accounts in recent years, persons have reported experiences of seeming to leave their bodies in what might be described as a death, but they lived to tell about it. Reports are similar of entering a tunnel of darkness, then being met by a bright light or presence in a setting so beautiful they didn't want to leave.

Whether they were actually in the portals of heaven has been argued and is unclear. What happens to a person in the first moments after death is widely discussed and is really unknown. It is not really clear, even from the Bible.

What is clear is that we do not have to wait for the eternal kind of life to begin at death. For Christians it begins *here and now.* In Jesus's preaching, he announced that the kingdom of God has come (Matt. 4:17; 10:5–8). In *The Divine Conspiracy,* Dallas Willard says that Jesus came to make known the open availability of life in the kingdom of God, here and now.

Bodily death is merely a brief transition to a new location. A friend of mine prefers to refer to a death as "passing," rather than "passing away." An aged acquaintance said that at times when in fellowship with God, the veil between the present and the beyond became so thin that he couldn't tell if he was still alive on earth or had entered the beyond.

Whatever the sequence of events at death, we can be assured that we will be in the care of the same loving God with whom we have become deeply acquainted in our earthly life.

—Leroy Brightup

Song: "Face to Face"

A Suggested Prayer: Thy kingdom come, thy will be done in my life here and now.

What Is Heaven Like?

Bible Reading: Revelation 4:5–11

As we age, we think more about the end of our life, which we know is coming. When in his early eighties, my father told me, "I've been talking to the Lord about my death." The story is told of a child who raised the question as to why the elderly grandmother read her Bible so much. Another child responded, "She is studying for final exams!"

A widespread fiction depicts heaven as a place where the departed float lazily on billowy clouds, strumming harps. Those who know something about the Bible often envision images from the book of Revelation, of people walking on streets of gold and wearing crowns. These descriptions in Revelation are an earthly picture depicting the best and most beautiful that can be imagined.

In reality, heaven will have to do very little with materialistic attire and street improvements. Actually, the book of Revelation focuses more on what goes on in heaven than what it looks like. It will have everything to do with relationships in the presence of the God we've come to know and love. A Bill Gaither song expresses the sentiment that God grows "sweeter" with the length of years together. Heaven will be an extension of this life romance.

Revelation contains numerous scenes of saints and angels gathered around the throne of God, lifting praise and adoration, enthralled by his grace and love, especially in chapters four and five. Even people who never considered themselves singers in this life will lift their voices to the joyful "Holy, holy, holy" and "Worthy art thou our Lord."

—Leroy Brightup

Song: "The Longer I Serve Him"

A Suggested Prayer: "To him who sits on the throne, and to the Lamb, be blessing and honor and glory and dominion forever and ever" (Revelation 5:13 [NASB]).

Works Cited

Books

Foster, Richard J. *Celebration of Discipline.* San Francisco: Harper & Row, 1978.

_____ . *Prayer.* San Francisco: Harper, 1992.

Juengst, Sara Covin. *Like a Garden.* Louisville: Westminster John Knox Press, 1996.

McCoy, Faye Bertholf. *One Generation Shall Praise Thy Works to Another.* Wichita, Kansas: Larksfield Press, 2003. Provided as a public service of *Witness to History*, A Program of the Cramer Reed Center for Successful Aging. (Cited as *One Generation*)

Mullen, Tom. *Living Longer and Other Sobering Possibilities.* Richmond, Indiana: Friends United Press, 1996. (Cited as *Living Longer)*

Poole, Joan N. and Viola Britt, eds. *Refreshings.* Greensboro, NC: North Carolina Yearly Meeting, 1990.

Smith, James Bryan. *Embracing the Love of God.* San Francisco: Harper, 1995.

Tengbom, Mildred. *Moving into a New Now.* Minneapolis: Augsburg, 1997. (Cited as *Moving*)

Willard, Dallas. *The Divine Conspiracy.* San Francisco: Harper, 1998.

Winn, Harold B. *Friend to Friend.* Salem, Ohio: Lyle Printing and Publishing Co., n.d.

Articles, Journals, and Periodicals

Fruit of the Vine. Vol. 40, No. 3 (July, August, September 2000). Newberg, Oregon: Barclay Press. (Cited as *Fruit*, vol. 40, no. 3)

Fruit of the Vine. Vol. 49, No. 3 (July, August, September 2009). Newberg, Oregon: Barclay Press. (Cited as *Fruit*, vol. 49, no. 3)

Fruit of the Vine. Vol. 49, No. 4 (October, November, December 2009). Newberg, Oregon: Barclay Press. (Cited as *Fruit*, vol. 49, no. 4)

Furr, Ruth E. "The Long Way Home," *Everyday Stewardship.* Vol. 43, No. 3 (Fall 2009), pp. 11–13. Goshen, Indiana: Mennonite Mutual Aid. (Cited as *Stewardship*)

Ross, Loretta F. *Holy Ground.* Vol. 19, No. 4 (Winter 2009), pp. 1–6. Topeka, Kansas: The Sanctuary Foundation for Prayer.

Weavings (published quarterly) Nashville: The Upper Room.

Index of Contributors

Made in United States
Orlando, FL
17 March 2023

31121881R00145